MICHAEL WIESE PRODUCTIONS
www.mwp.com

Since 1981, Michael Wiese Productions has been dedicated to providing novice and seasoned filmmakers with vital information on all aspects of filmmaking and videomaking. We have published more than 50 books, used in over 500 film schools worldwide.

Our authors are successful industry professionals — they believe that the more knowledge and experience they share with others, the more high-quality films will be made. That's why they spend countless hours writing about the hard stuff: budgeting, financing, directing, marketing, and distribution. Many of our authors, including myself, are often invited to conduct filmmaking seminars around the world.

We truly hope that our publications, seminars, and consulting services will empower you to create enduring films that will last for generations to come.

We're here to help. Let us hear from you.

Sincerely,

Michael Wiese
Publisher, Filmmaker

SCREENWRITING ON THE INTERNET

Researching, Writing, and Selling
Your Script on the Web

by
Christopher Wehner

Published by Michael Wiese Productions
11288 Ventura Blvd., Suite 821
Studio City, CA 91604
tel. (818) 379- 8799
fax (818) 986-3408
mw@mwp.com
www.mwp.com

Cover Design: Alexander Arkadin
Book Layout: Gina Mansfield

Printed by McNaughton & Gunn, Inc., Saline, Michigan
Manufactured in the United States of America

ISBN 0-941188-36-1

Library of Congress Cataloging-in-Publication Data

Wehner, Christopher, 1969–
    Screenwriting on the internet: researching, writing, and selling your script on the web/ by Christopher Wehner.
        p. cm.
    ISBN 0-941188-36-1
      1. Motion picture authorship. 2. Motion picture authorship—Computer network resources. I. Title.

PN1996 .W294 2001
808.2'3'0285—dc21   2001035767
                                                                      CIP

For Mom

TABLE OF CONTENTS

SPECIAL ACKNOWLEDGMENTS

You need family support whenever you try to accomplish anything meaningful. I'd like to let my loving wife, sister, father, uncle, grandmother, and children know how much their support has meant. I couldn't have done it without you guys.

PROFESSIONAL ACKNOWLEDGMENTS

Syd Field, Richard Finney, Thom Taylor, Frederick Levy, Adam Kline, Ed Kashiba, Dave Trottier, Michael Grace, Michael B. Druxman, Kenna McHugh, Don Vasicek, Daniel Knauf, Howard Meibach, Brent Armitage, Tony Urban, Karen Kinsman, Steve Alten, Mark Atwater, Michael McPherson, Craig Griffin, Scott Frank, Chris Oxley, Harry Preston, Jenna Glatzer, Neill D. Hicks, Charles Deemer, Andy Cohen, Jill Nowak, Andrea Leigh Wolf, Bud Fleisher, Jonathan Zaleski, and the many writers whom I have encountered on the Internet who shared with me their stories and knowledge. Thanks to everyone.

INTRODUCTION

"You can take Hollywood for granted like I did, or you can dismiss it with the contempt we reserve for what we don't understand."

— F. Scott Fitzgerald,
The Last Tycoon

In 1995 I established a Web site called Screenwriters Utopia.[1] It was a very simple place, no more than a dozen pages. It reflected the Internet of its day — mostly made up of text, without a lot of graphics.

The Internet has become a vastly different place from the one that I first encountered in the early 1990s. Looking back over the last few years, it's pretty incredible what the implications of the Internet's growth have been in terms of the economic, commercial, and social effects. (The Internet has actually been around since the 1970s, and its origins go back even farther... but that's another book.)

My "ideal place" for screenwriters was a means to an end for me personally. I was a struggling writer, hated my day job, and loathed the direction my professional life was heading. (Thankfully I have a loving and supportive wife.) I realized I had to start over. So I did. I learned how to use the Web to my advantage, and I discovered that it could help me obtain my goals as a writer. Along the way I realized there were a lot of other writers out there just like me. The Screenwriters Utopia became a gathering place for all screenwriters, and it soon began to flourish.

Though the demands of running a Web site limited my writing schedule I still managed to find time. I eventually signed with an agent, optioned a couple of screenplays, and became a published author, none of which would have happened without the Internet. I am a firm believer that the

---

[1] *www.screenwritersutopia.com*

Web can help every one of you succeed. And the best part is, I don't have to waste half this book trying to prove it to you, because I am the proof.

My little Web site has grown to more than 3,000 pages and nearly 100,000 monthly visitors — not bad for just a screenwriting Web site. I now work entirely on the Web as an editor, manager, and writer.

THE INFORMATION SUPER-TRAFFIC JAM

The Information Superhighway has become the *Information Super-Traffic Jam*. There is simply too much information that is too readily available. I am going to simplify it for you. I have purposely strayed clear of writing another instructional manual on screenwriting. This book is not going to provide much how-to information for writing a screenplay.

This book is about empowerment. The techniques and coaching I provide will only get you halfway there; your ability, talent, and desire will have to do the rest. I want you to help yourself. Do not rely on any one person's advice. There is no one right or wrong way. There are no formulas for success. I'm going to offer guidance and a helping hand. The resources and Web sites within these pages can help you research, write, and sell your screenplay online.

WHAT'S INSIDE THE BOOK?

In Chapter One, you can read a few short stories about screenwriting on the Internet. These anecdotes are reflections of success and disappointment as told by the writers who experienced them. It is my hope that this chapter will both inspire and warn you before you begin your journey.

Next up is *Researching on the Internet*, Chapter Two. Here we roll up our sleeves and get to work. This chapter is intended for the unschooled Internet user. However, experienced surfers may still want to skim through it as well. Doing research for your screenplay is the first step.

Often you'll find that some research will be required before you can start writing. Also in this chapter, I offer some very specific resources dealing with selected topics and categories, including "Serial Killers" and "Crime Scene Technology," along with information on how to search the Web effectively.

Chapter Three deals with *Screenwriting Resources*. Here, I break down these resources into areas for beginner, intermediate, and ready-to-sell screenwriters. I'll point you to resources that will help you learn the very basics of screenwriting, as well as advance your knowledge of the craft. Whatever your needs, I hope you will find some direction in this chapter.

The E-mail Query is the subject of Chapter Four. When you sit down to write an e-mail query, you need to give it serious thought. There is a developing system, and there are some guidelines that you should know. I've been contacting producers and agents with e-mail since 1995, and I have had a lot of success. A few years ago I offered a short article on my Web site that dealt with e-mail queries. I think it was one of the first on the subject, and I received an enormous amount of feedback. That experience is really the impetus for this book. Just like the written query letter, the quality of your e-mail query will make or break you.

In Chapter Five, I discuss *Agents & Agencies*, and provide a select listing. As an aspiring screenwriter, obtaining a good agent can make all the difference in the world. Unfortunately, the reality is that getting a quality agent will be one of the most difficult tasks you'll ever face.

Chapter Six deals with *Producers & Production Companies*. You need to understand producers, and what it is they are trying to achieve. I think what you'll find is that the two of you are really not all that different. This chapter also includes a large listing of Web addresses and e-mails of producers you can contact.

Script Sites are everywhere now. Some just want your money and really offer nothing in return. Can these sites really help you sell your material? Who are they, what do they do, and why should you use them? These are just a few of the questions I'll answer in Chapter Seven.

Chapter Eight examines the precarious position *Script Consultants* find themselves in today. Some are having a hard time holding up under the onslaught of script sites. In this chapter we'll take a look at online consultants, what they offer, and how they can help you.

The next chapter deals with marketing. It is really the culmination of several chapters in this book that lead up to what I discuss here. You're not just an artist; you have to be savvy and understand how to promote yourself and your material. I've had to learn how to do this, and I know you can too. In Chapter Nine, I discuss *Marketing Your Screenplay*. I have some tips and suggestions for you as you set out to sell your script.

Conducting the interviews for this book was the most enjoyable part for me. In Chapter Ten, you can read a few select interviews from my research. Reading what a professional writer, producer, or script consultant has to say will be instrumental as you find your way through *Screenwriting on the Internet*.

[For updates on this book, please check *www.netscreenwriter.com*]

CHAPTER ONE

SCREENWRITING ON THE INTERNET

"As long as I can remember I've wanted to be a writer. When my family would leave for weekend outings, I would stay home and write. I'm not sure I'd recommend it to everyone, but it worked for me. The only way I've been able to progress within my craft is to work at it for years."

— Richard Finney, professional screenwriter

"... to work at it for years." While researching this book, I was struck by how many writers thought that success was not only sure to come, but would come quickly. The Web itself is partly to blame. On the one hand, it has leveled the playing field for new writers in search of success. Aspiring screenwriters, no matter where they are, really do have a chance at selling a script. On the other hand, its very nature breeds the mentality that everything is easy and free.

The Internet offers everything from free software to free news and information. And if you're willing to put up with some advertising, you can get free e-mail and even free Internet access. If you're a struggling screenwriter, I can only assume that money is an issue for you. And that would be a big reason why the Web should be such an important part of your daily activities.

Screenwriting on the Internet can be a harrowing experience. You will run into a lot of different people. Some are only after your money, but in my experience the majority of professionals and companies out there are legitimate. They all have a common interest. They all want admission into "the game," and they need a great script to do it. You just might be the next great screenwriter, and they know it. It's not always easy to know what to do, but sometimes you have to take a chance.

1

With that in mind, I want to share a few stories and reflections with you. I hope they inspire you to reach for your dreams and warn you of possible danger. But mostly, I hope you find something to help you as you navigate your way around cyberspace.

AN INTERNET COLLABORATION

Tony Urban and Michael Addis, co-writers of *Poor White Trash*, had not met face to face until the day before their movie was to start filming, yet they had managed to collaborate on the screenplay and sell it.

Living in Pennsylvania, struggling screenwriter Tony Urban was constantly surfing the Net querying producers and directors in an effort to garner interest in his "spec" (speculative) script *Sticks and Stones*. "I e-mailed everyone who was in any way associated with the film industry: writers, directors, crew, actors, grips, anyone I could find an e-mail address for. You never know when a 'nobody' is going to send you in the right direction," recalls Urban.

But for the longest time it seemed that no one was interested in his script, so he started work on another idea, *Poor White Trash*. Then one day he came across a Web site for director Michael Addis. "I had just started writing *Poor White Trash* and gave him a pitch."

Michael Addis lived in Los Angeles and worked as a writer/director of short films and music videos. He was frustrated with his career every bit as much as Tony Urban was with his. Though he was a successful director of short films with numerous awards to his credit, he really wanted to make feature films. What should have been his first effort, *Die Wholesale*, was at that time bogged down in a serious legal battle.

Addis liked Urban's idea enough to ask whether he could co-write it with him. Tony didn't bat an eyelash. He began sending Addis his notes. "I was naive and never even considered the possibility of being ripped off," said Urban.

That makes this story even more remarkable. Most writers in Tony's position would have been skeptical and distrustful. Most other writers would never have gone for it.

"I'd advise other writers in partnerships to sign contracts. When it came time for the William Morris Agency to send the script around, Michael and I did finalize everything in writing. Even with friends, when it comes to money, it's just too much of a risk not to," Urban now admits.

Using only e-mail, they began writing the script together. "Michael and I created a very in-depth outline/treatment, breaking down every single scene," said Urban. "Then we split the script in half. He took the first part, I took the second, and we wrote it in a few days. The next few months were spent polishing."

All of this was accomplished online and with e-mail. Addis' agent at William Morris then took the script and began showing it around. It was not long after, when Kingsize Entertainment made an offer to Addis and Urban, which included Addis directing the film.

Then in July of 1999, near the set of the film, it happened: Tony Urban and Michael Addis met for the first time. "I'd driven from Pennsylvania to Benton, Illinois (where the movie was filming) — a ten-and-a-half-hour haul. Misery! I stopped at the hotel and called Michael at the production office. No one else was in. That was around six in the morning. He later swung by in a van, and we were off to do rewrites." Of course, the meeting included a friendly smile and a handshake!

TOMORROW'S WISH

"Without the writer there would be no stories. And yet most of the time new writers are not treated with respect."
— Karen Kinsman

Karen Kinsman lives in Perry, Maine, which by her own admission is a "very remote spot." She had spent her days helping her husband, who's an artist, with his work. But for years a story kept haunting her. Eventually this led to her putting it down on paper.

"When I wrote the story it was more or less a personal experience. I never intended to sell it. I wrote it as a way to heal. I wanted to work through certain things in the past, and what I ended up with was a novel," says Karen. "It's a nostalgic drama of passion and betrayal. A love triangle between a woman and two brothers... a coming of age story, really, based on truth."

The unpublished novel is called *Tomorrow's Wish*, named after a song written by her father, who was a country singer.

She poured her heart and soul into over 500 pages in her first draft. She then spent six months refining, shaping, and molding it into a salable story.

During one long and cold winter, she and her husband traveled south to see some old friends and to thaw out a bit. While there she showed her manuscript to a friend of her husband's, actor James Gammon of *Nash Bridges*. James thought it would make a great television Movie of the Week. On his advice, she adapted her novel into a screenplay. "I wrote the screenplay in about a month," says Karen.

Once the script was completed, the next logical step was to find an agent, "someone who could help me and who knows the business," recalls Karen. "I started querying agents, but I didn't have any luck. I found it was difficult to get an agent. Soon I began searching the Internet."

After awhile she came across *storybay.com*, a fee-based service that provides aspiring screenwriters with script coverage, and for exceptional screenplays, seeks a buyer from a network of agency and production-company partners in the Hollywood community. She paid the required fee ($150 at the time) and sent in her screenplay.

"I took a chance and submitted. I didn't know what would happen," recalls Karen. Within a month she learned that her script received high marks and would be available for producers and agents to review.

Not long after, Canada's Millbrook Productions discovered Karen's script on *storybay.com* and offered her an option. Not only was she going to be a professional screenwriter, but she had the savvy to negotiate to be the executive producer on the project.

"Storybay set it all up and had everything arranged," reflects Karen, "right down to the signing of the option. They went over the agreement with me line by line. Being a new writer, I was amazed. Who would have thought I would be optioned!"

Within a few weeks of signing the agreement, Karen was off to Florida for a much-deserved vacation. "I'm working on my second screenplay," Karen told me. "So it will be a working vacation, but with some warm weather."

BREAKING INTO FILM

Kenna McHugh is an author, screenwriter, and producer who has worked in video, television, and film. As far as working the Web goes, she's been online as long as anyone. She has been writing for my Web site since 1997 and has made a nice income on the side, writing for various publications and Web sites. Her story alone is a success, but when I spoke with her for this book I was struck by a story she told me — one where she got the chance to help out someone else who was trying to start a career.

Not long after Kenna's book, *Breaking into Film*, came out in 1999, she received an e-mail from a young woman who wanted to become a director. "She e-mailed and asked if I knew how she could get work in film," explained Kenna. "I told her about a book signing I was doing for *Breaking into Film*, and to come on by and talk. She took me up on it, we met, and we exchanged numbers.

"Later, I called her up and asked her to help me out with a project I was producing. She did. I observed that she was reliable, hard-working, and had a great attitude for the business. About a year later, I was offered a job to work on a John Travolta film. I couldn't because I was committed to another project. But, I recommended this young woman. She got the job, worked with Nora Ephron, and launched her career in the film business.

"The point is that she took the initiative to surf the Internet, find me, and contact me, and now she's working in the business with a goal to be a director. Ironically, she is from my [home] town."

A BUNCH OF HILLBILLIES...

I had three finished screenplays, and for what seemed like forever I had been submitting log lines and e-mail queries to dozens and dozens of contacts. Then one day I finally got an excited response from a real live producer with real credits, who had just read my script and really seemed to like it.

"This is one of the best scripts I've read lately. It's edgy, smart, and you really take some chances with your story. I get scripts from CAA that aren't this good." As he said those magical words, I was imagining myself riding down Hollywood Boulevard in my new Porsche, with the top down so my hair could blow in the warm California air. He rambled on for another minute or two. To this day, I have no idea what he said.

I remember snapping out of it as he told me I should have an answering machine. He apparently had tried to call earlier, and no one answered. I told him I couldn't afford one.

After a moment of silence he continued, "Listen, can you overnight me a clean copy so I can show it to my agent and a couple of directors by the weekend?"

"Can't you just make copies?" I replied. After all, didn't I just tell him I couldn't afford a thirty-dollar answering machine? Now he was asking me to spend fifteen dollars for overnight delivery.

"I wrote notes all over this one," he explained.

"Oh," I said.

So I paid the fifteen bucks and some change to FedEx a clean copy for next-day delivery. He further explained that he wanted his agent and a couple of "director friends" to look at it before he offered me any kind of option. "Great, good, great," I replied, or something like that.

Needless to say, I was riding high. I blew off my job and went down to a local car dealership that handles sports cars and started test-driving them all. I was going to be an optioned screenwriter.

It was about two weeks later when panic set in. Nary a phone call or e-mail came my way. But I wasn't going to be deterred. I just knew he was going to call with good news "any minute now."

When I finally got hold of him, he told me that he decided to go in a "different direction." Apparently his agent and director friend didn't respond to the script as he had hoped. "Besides," he said, followed by a pause, "after re-reading it, your dialogue in some places sounds like a bunch of hillbillies — and the ending, I mean, it would never play on the big screen."

"I'll rewrite that part!"

"Sorry, kid." He hung up.

So much for my "edgy, smart" script that he loved just a few weeks ago. This was my first lesson in the realities of the business. I have no doubt that he really did like my script at first, just as I have no doubt that later on he really did not.

FROM NOWHERE TO MEL GIBSON IN SIX DAYS

"To go from nowhere to Mel Gibson in six days, it was a roller coaster ride. It was horrible," says former Colorado dude ranch owner Mark L. Smith with a laugh. "When Bruce Willis was attached they said, 'It's a done deal. Just wait.' So I waited."

Then word came down that MGM, who was considering the project for Willis, had passed. The script in question was a Western — they didn't like that part. They wanted it changed. That's when Sherry Lansing, Chairman and CEO of Paramount, apparently read the script and considered the project for Mel Gibson and his production company, Icon.

"I got the call late that night. They said, 'Wait up an hour, we're going to have great news for you,'" recalls Mark wryly. "So I waited an hour, then two, but no call. Finally, I called them." Never a good sign when you have to do the calling.

"They told me it fell through. It was like that, until it finally did sell a day later. It was truly an exciting experience, and one I'm sure anyone would like to have."

In late February, 2001, Mark not only sold his script, *The Devil's Kiss*, but has several more projects getting looked at with names like Brad Pitt and Bruce Willis interested — all of which was accomplished online, and without the help of an agent.

A very unassuming person and down-to-earth, Mark is the kind of writer you could easily end up rooting for and certainly admire. "For the whole thing to happen so fast, I don't know, maybe that's how they work out there. I just didn't know enough about it I guess," says Mark, reflecting on his six-years-in-the-making overnight success story.

As a kid Mark was hooked the first time he saw *Butch Cassidy and the Sundance Kid*. "William Goldman is probably the closest thing to a hero I have as a writer. His writing pulled me into the movies," admits Mark.

When Mark began his screenwriting career he was still a dude ranch owner in Colorado, and despite the demands that come with it he was able to produce some quality writing. "The very first thing I wrote I entered in the Nicholl Fellowship contest, and it ended up a semi-finalist," recalls Mark. "A producer saw it and took it to Disney. She pitched it to them as the next great family movie. They liked it, but thought it was too old-style. It was kind of a family adventure movie about two brothers."

As aspiring screenwriters know, there can be long dry spells between hits from the occasional producer or agent. Mark used this time wisely by attending events and workshops at AFI (American Film Institute). "I stayed there for a few months, trying to absorb as much as I could about structure and everything else. I eventually optioned a couple scripts to some small companies, but could never get in the loop."

Optioning material, having a couple "near misses," could be called a career for some aspiring screenwriters. Mark was only motivated to work harder.

Around this time he and his wife sold their dude ranch and moved closer to her family in North Carolina. Barely allowing time to unpack and settle into his new home, Mark continued writing. What he ended up with was *The Devil's Kiss*, a story that deals with a sheriff who is about to retire, but must stay on and help his new replacement solve a string of grisly and mysterious murders. After completion Mark sent it to a manager he knew in L.A.

"He thought it was good, but since it was set in the West, a kind of Western, he felt there was nothing he could do with it. So it sat on his desk for months. I just believed that it was good enough that something should happen to it." That's when Mark turned to the Internet.

"Six years ago, when I first started, there just weren't the options [online] there are now. It's incredible what's out there today."

Eventually Mark stumbled onto *scriptshark.com*, a script service company. He decided to give them a try. "I sent in *The Devil's Kiss*, just to get the [coverage] notes mainly," says Mark. "I didn't really know much about them. When I got the coverage it was very good. They called and asked to post it in their 'Spec Market.'"

Mark was curious enough that he allowed ScriptShark to post his coverage. It would end up being a good move on his part.

"Bender-Spink was one of the first to call and ask to get a copy. Ed Kashiba, who runs ScriptShark, got it over to them immediately. They ended up going wide with it, and at one point Bruce Willis was attached, then they were even talking to Clint Eastwood, and eventually it ended up with Icon and Paramount six days later." Mel Gibson's Icon Productions ended up forking over a low six figures for *The Devil's Kiss*.

In six days Mark went from "Joe Nobody" to "Joe Somebody," and it most likely would never have happened without the Internet.

"I had actually placed a deadline on myself," says Mark after a moment of thought. "It would have been six years in May, and I thought that was long enough. It obviously wasn't going to happen. ScriptShark saved me; it couldn't have happened at a better time."

"Hopefully my query letter days are gone."

"I think so," I replied.

THE WRITER GOT SCREWED!

A post on a message board, "Writers Wanted," is all it takes. "The post was pretty simple: Send script, no money or fees, and they'll determine if it has 'merit,'" recalls one writer.

So he sent in his script, and about three or four days later he heard from them. The so-called agent said he liked the writing, thought it had "potential," and wondered if the writer would be open to rewrites. "I was very excited. Here was someone who mattered that liked my writing," the writer told me.

The first warning sign was there, but it was hard to see. The fact that it only took three or four days to get a reply should make you suspicious. The package probably took that long just to arrive. As soon as it did, this person was on the phone back to the writer, most likely without even reading the script.

The agent then said that he wanted the script to be "read professionally" to make sure that the concerns and notes he had about the story were right. "He told me that it would cost 750 dollars. I was in shock, yet I really wanted this to happen," he said.

He sent out his check. Weeks passed, and not a word came from the "agent." The phone number he had been given was soon disconnected.

POP QUIZ: WHAT DO YOU DO?

You're a desperate writer who can barely pay your bills. You have only $48 in your checking account. Your only major possessions are an old 1971 Malibu convertible your dad bought for you when you were seventeen and an out-of-date computer — you most certainly don't own a home. On the plus side, you've got a loving wife, three kids, and a job. Not bad for most people, but writers aren't like most people.

After sending out numerous queries, you receive a positive response from a Los Angeles agency, AEI.[1] You decide to send them your only finished product, a tale about a prehistoric shark. The story is called *MEG*. A few weeks later they call you. They want to help you develop your story and get your characters worked out. But there's a catch: they say it'll cost you $6,000.[2] They also tell you they can't guarantee they will sell your story, but they have connections and can get your project into some major companies like Walt Disney. What do you do?

As if there were any doubts: You run for the hills and never look back.

But, if you're Steve Alten, you sell your car and go for it. "I didn't know AEI, but they were the only ones who believed in my work. I hated my job and knew something had to change. It is easier to take chances when you are desperate, which I was," reflects Steve.

"To be successful in any field requires calculated risk and lots of effort and belief. Some nights I was so tired I literally fell asleep on the keyboard. But nothing worth having comes easy. And in my mind, I kept imagining

---

[1]AEI (Atichity Editorial/Entertainment International, Inc.) is run by Ken Atchity. They are a full-service literary management and motion picture production company. You can find AEI online at *www.lainet.com/~aeikja/*.
[2]The $6,000 fee was due to the fact that *MEG* was an unfinished manuscript at the time. AEI worked with Mr. Alten to develop a significant portion of the work.

11

going to the world premiere of *MEG*. I still imagine it every time I see a movie," says Steve.

"By September — Friday the 13th — I arrived at my job only to learn that I had been laid off," recalls Steve. "I returned home broke, with $48 in the bank and bills due. Four days later, AEI had a bidding war going for *MEG*. Three weeks later, all of my bills were paid in full."

SOME VERY NICE REJECTIONS

Within weeks of my most recent rejection, an agent whom I had contacted via the Web wanted to represent me after reading one of my screenplays. This agent resided in Bel Air and seemed very legit. Her name was Brenda, and she wanted me to do some rewriting — the warning light went on — but she wanted her assistant, who was an accomplished screenwriter, to help me. No cost, no nothing. So I spent several months working with Joanne (Brenda's assistant) on the script. It was an incredible experience, and the script was much improved. They knew what they were doing.

Soon it was time to start sending out the script. It was probably one of the most exciting times of my life. They had several companies lined up to read it: Dino De Laurentiis, New Line Cinema, Miramax and others. I was riding pretty high, only this time I didn't allow myself to daydream or test-drive sports cars.

Days then weeks had passed when word came that the script was generating no heat whatsoever. I did get some very nice rejections, or so they tell me. Within a couple of months I couldn't get Brenda or Joanne to return an e-mail, let alone a phone call. I was down in the dumps again.

OF PLANES, E-MAILS & WEB SITES...

You never know when opportunity will come calling. Mark Atwater was on his way home from Los Angeles, where he had just finished several meetings with producers with whom he had made contact over the Web.

"[On the flight] I met Tim Flattery, an illustrator and concept designer for such films as *A.I.*, *The Sixth Day*, and *Unbreakable*. He sat right next to me, and we talked nearly the whole four-hour flight," recalls Mark. "I told him about myself and my projects, not really thinking anything would come from it."

Mark runs an extremely popular Web site called Mark's Screenwriting Page,[3] where he holds chat sessions every week. "There isn't exactly a burgeoning screenwriting community where I live," says Mark, "so the chat has been the best outlet for meeting and talking craft with other writers."

Mark has made all of his contacts — well almost all — from his Web site or through e-mail queries saying, "I've completed ten screenplays, I've had three of those screenplays optioned, and I've written one screenplay for hire. In a large part, the Internet has helped me start my career from the middle of nowhere [Illinois]."

Mark arrived home from his L.A. adventure and got back to the daily grind. A couple of months passed and his conversations with Tim Flattery were totally forgotten when out of the blue he got a call. It was Flattery, who finally had a chance to contact Mark about one of his stories. "Tim said he was interested in reading *Shortkill*," recalls Mark. "Six days later he called back and said he wanted to option it and direct it himself. That Sunday I received the contract."

NOBODY BREATHE

Michael McPherson is certainly a veteran when it comes to screenwriting on the Internet. "I've been using the Web to establish contacts for four or five years now," says Michael.

He's not just an aspiring screenwriter. Success has finally come knocking for him. He's won numerous screenwriting contests and has a film in development. His script, *Against Their Will*, is set to start filming in the spring of 2001. Produced by Alex Michaels, COO of

---

[3] *www.geocities.com/Hollywood/Theater/6448/*

Prelude Productions, it will be shot digitally. "I even have an agent now, a WGA signatory at that... so I suppose things are looking up," concludes Michael.

When speaking with a veteran of the Web such as Michael, you get an immediate sense of reserved confidence. The Web is helping so many writers get their feet in the door, but like Michael, they are finding that it takes time.

Before success there is almost always disappointment. Michael's action script, *Nobody Breathe*, appeared on the verge of being produced. "They gave me a song and dance routine for over a year," recalls Michael, "promised to send a check or forward back an option agreement that I had changed and wanted them to agree to. I put the pressure on and kept bugging them for something concrete. Finally, they stopped corresponding altogether.

"I later found a Web page where they had changed the story line of the script, something they did not tell me about. I mean, here they were advertising something for future development — my script with changes — and they hadn't even signed an option agreement with me!"

FINDING YOUR BEARINGS

Ups and downs, peaks and valleys, what else should anyone really expect? No longer can we say the Internet is the future; it's the here and now. It doesn't matter if you're ready or not because, like it or not, almost all of you are going to need it — in some form — to succeed as a screenwriter. If anything, the Internet has become too busy and a little overwhelming, but its weaknesses are also its strengths. As you navigate your way around, you'll learn what works best and discard what does not. You'll eventually find your bearings.

CHAPTER TWO

RESEARCHING ON THE INTERNET

Surfing the Internet is like having the world's largest library at your fingertips. However, if you're not sagacious enough to find what you're looking for, it can be like standing at the base of a mountain of information, peering up at endless levels of books and periodicals, without a clue as to where to begin. You need to find the right information, and you need to find it fairly quickly.

Even professional writers spend time doing research online. "I do research on the subject matter that I am working on with my projects," says professional screenwriter Don Vasicek (*Warriors of Virtue, Born to Win*). "I'm continually amazed at the massiveness of available information on the Web. It's awesome to me." But not all of us can be as lucky as prolific author Elmore Leonard (*Get Shorty, Out Of Sight*), who has his own research assistant. Unfortunately for you and me, we'll have to do our own research.

For example, you might need information on how a murder scene is processed by police. You'll want to research everything from procedures to the technical language that is used. Every aspect of your story that requires knowledge you do not possess should be investigated. Don't just make stuff up. There is no excuse to not know what it is you're talking about when you write your screenplay.

SOME BASICS

When searching on the Web, you need to use the right keywords and ask the right questions, but that's not all. There are a couple of different strategies that can be applied. Consider the following questions: Do you know what a Boolean search is? Why is it important to use quotation marks when you're searching for a phrase? These are simple questions, but very important ones.

SEARCH TIPS

- Have a strategy in mind. Are you looking for a phrase, or would a single keyword be sufficient?
- Be sure to determine the variations and synonyms for the keyword(s) you are using and incorporate those into your phrase as needed. Also, make sure you have the correct spelling and definition.
- Finally, are you really seeking the answer to a question? This is a perfect example of when you'll need quotation marks. There is also a nice device called *askjeeves.com* that will take your question and display the most appropriate Web sites for you to find the answer.

THE BOOLEAN SEARCH

To put it simply, Boolean searching involves three words: AND, OR, and NOT. In order to use these words correctly you have to understand the logic behind Boolean. Think in terms of a math equation, and a very basic one at that: *word plus word minus word*. For example, "nuclear AND war NOT cold." With *altavista.com* (see below) I have more success using the actual + and − symbols: "nuclear + war − cold."

You can also use the OR command, which essentially tells the searching device to look for pages containing either word "A" OR word "B" in your phrase.

Google.com makes Boolean searching very easy on their "Advanced Search" page by proposing a series of questions for you to answer. If you know what you're looking for, have a strategy, and understand the words you're using, you should do very well in your search.[1]

QUOTATION MARKS

When you're searching for a question or a phrase use quotation marks. They

---

[1] Vicky Phillips & Cindy Yager, *Writer's Guide to Internet Resources.* Macmillian, New York: 1998, 225–226.

can make a big difference when searching. Some searching devices automatically search for phrases, but to be safe, use quotations. Once again, always consult the "Advanced Search" options of a search engine.

WHERE TO START?

SEARCH ENGINES

When doing research, the obvious starting point is a search engine, but it matters which one you select. There are just a few I use with any kind of regularity. I want good results, not a lot of junk returned when I search.

google.com

Do not be fooled by the simple presentation of this search engine. It is one of the most powerful devices on the Web. At the time of this writing it has over one billion Web sites indexed. For example, using a keyword search I type "autopsy." The third result I get is The Johns Hopkins Autopsy Resource at *ww2.med.jhu.edu/pathology/iad.html*. From there I am on my way.

altavista.com

This is another great search engine. You can browse by category or jump right in with a search query. If you're looking for information on a specific topic like "crime," then try their category listings first.

Do You Yahoo?

Yahoo.com is a directory. It does not spider sites like search engines.[2] When you submit your personal home page to Yahoo, it will take longer for it to get listed. The reason is that Yahoo manually indexes Web sites and by doing so maintains the best directory of categories on the Web. If you're looking for some information on say, "forensics," Yahoo has a category for it and many more.

---

[2] Spiders are automated devices that crawl around the Web collecting links for search engines.

Nueva Library Help Page —
nuevaschool.org/~debbie/library/research/adviceengine.html
If these searching devices (above) are just not helping, try this neat page compiled by Debbie Abilock. The type of information you are looking for is cross-referenced with the proper searching device, whether it be a search engine, directory, or database. It's a great place to start your research.

Internet Search FAQ — *www.purefiction.com/pages/res1.html*
If you're still having trouble figuring out where to start, take a visit to this site. It is as comprehensive a guide for doing research on the Web as I have found. It is an excellent resource that is updated regularly.

THE INVISIBLE WEB

Though search engines are the best places to start your research, they are not by any means the last and only option. There are dictionaries and encyclopedias that you might want to consult as well. I list some of these below. However, there are databases and Web pages that cannot be indexed by spiders, which means most search engines do not list them. So in essence there are some areas of the Web that are "invisible" to a lot of people who only use search engines when doing research.

The Invisible Web — *www.invisibleweb.com*
I wasn't even aware there was an "invisible Web" until I came across this site. The Invisible Web is a directory of over 10,000 databases, Web pages, and searching devices that cannot be indexed by standard Internet search engines.

REFERENCES AND ENCYCLOPEDIAS

Some of the biggest casualties of the Internet are those old encyclopedia sets. Mine was a family heirloom. Not only were they continually out-dated and inconvenient, they also took up an entire row of valuable bookshelf space. I wouldn't even consider buying another set with the resources that are available online. The Web is more convenient and is always updated. Even if you have to pay a small monthly or yearly fee, it's worth it.

Encyclopedia — *www.encyclopedia.com*
This site conveniently places more than 14,000 articles from *The Concise Columbia Electronic Encyclopedia, Third Edition* in an online database, free of charge. The information is presented in small chunks and cross-referenced to several other sources.

Encyberpedia — *www.encyberpedia.com/cyberlinks/links/index.html*
This is a nice resource that I think is picking up steam and will eventually be excellent. It has dozens of categories organized in a Yahoo-like fashion. It's definitely worth a look.

RefDesk — *www.refdesk.com*
Another useful site to get you pointed in the right direction quickly, it contains daily features and updates, along with a FAQ section and recommended reference tools.

Encyclopedia Britannica — *www.britannica.com*
I don't even know if Britannica still bothers to publish a print edition. If they do, I'd have to ask why. Basic historical and biographical information on important figures in history seems to be what I use *britannica.com* for most often. Not only can you search through their encyclopedias, but you can also search the Web. *Britannica.com* has started indexing Web pages much like Yahoo does. You can also get free e-mail and free software downloads.

Theinfosphere — *www.theinfosphere.com*
With over 2,000 terms and definitions along with Web site listings, this site's information is organized alphabetically, including by categories and most popular searches.

Free Internet Encyclopedia — *clever.net/cam/enc/search.html*
This device categorizes Web resources in an encyclopedic manner. It is maintained by Clif Davis and Margaret Adamson Fincannon.

Jim's Word/Writer's Links — *redrival.com/bloxword/jimsbmks.html*
This is a very impressive collection of useful links for writers. Almost every imaginable category or topic is covered.

DICTIONARIES

Along with standard dictionaries, there are resources online that are category specific. I have found these dictionaries to be incredibly useful and fast. I can't remember the last time I even picked up a printed dictionary.

yourdictionary.com
This is one of the top dictionary and language resources on the Web.

dir.yahoo.com/reference/dictionaries
Virtually every online dictionary worth looking at is listed in Yahoo.

BIOGRAPHICAL INFORMATION

The Biographical Dictionary — *www.s9.com/biography*
Their database contains more than 28,000 important men and women in history. You can search by date of birth or death, positions held, professions, literary and artistic works, achievements, and almost any other keyword you can imagine.

LIBRARIES

There are a lot of excellent online libraries. Some require that you are a student or member, others do not. Much like dictionaries, there are category-specific libraries available, from physics to sports and almost everything else.

directory.google.com/Top/Reference/Libraries/
dir.yahoo.com/Reference/Libraries/

POPULAR TOPICS

You're writing a period piece and need to know how to describe your main character, who is twelve years old. You've got the hair, eyes and whatever else down, but what about his attire? Don't worry, just check out Historical Boys Clothing at *members.tripod.com/~histclo/*. It is sometimes incredible what you can find. Never assume that what you're looking for is too obscure or inconsequential, because it's not.

What follows are some popular topics that seem to pop up in many a screenplay. Of course, it would be impossible to cover every topic. If I do not cover a category you are interested in, please use the suggestions outlined earlier in this chapter to start your research.

AUTOPSY

The Johns Hopkins Autopsy Resource —
ww2.med.jhu.edu/pathology/iad.html
This archive is searchable. Simply type in "gunshot wound" and you'll get plenty of results to look over. Reading an autopsy report itself is interesting. For example, Autopsy No. 16467 states "GUNSHOT WOUND perforating left lobe, liver, stomach, pancreas, left kidney, diaphragm, left lung. There was a necrosis infarction of the liver, along

with intracapsular hemorrhage of the left kidney." If you cannot decipher these results, you can consult with the Unified Medical Language System (*www.nlm.nih.gov/research/umls/*), or seek help at the National Library of Medicine (*www.nlm.nih.gov*).

After you have reviewed some autopsies, you're now ready to incorporate that into your autopsy scene.

```
              CHARACTER NAME
     (Speaking into a handheld tape
     recorder)
     Victim has gunshot wound perforating
     the upper left lobe, liver, stomach,
     and left kidney.  There was massive
     hemorrhaging...
```

CONSPIRACY THEORIES

Numerous films have dealt with "conspiracy theories" in one form or another. Oliver Stone's *JFK* is probably the most well known of recent memory to base its entire story on such a theory.

The Smoking Gun — *www.thesmokinggun.com*
Using material obtained from government and law enforcement sources, as well as court files, their site contains what they call some of the most "cool, confidential, and quirky" information on the Web.

Encyclopedia of Conspiracies Home Page —
www.cruzio.com/~blackops/
This is an easy-to-use directory. Conspiracies are indexed in alphabetical order.

Conspiracy Net — *www.conspiracy-net.com*
At the time of this writing, they have indexed over 725 conspiracies, including 211 alien/UFO articles. This is a well-maintained and organized site that allows you to quickly search for what you're looking for or just browse the archives.

CRIME, CRIME SCENES & LAW ENFORCEMENT PROCEDURES

From criminal investigation to crime-scene technology and procedures, every bit of information you gather is important. Make your screenplay as professional as possible. Don't stop at just doing research; find some real-life detectives and ask them questions.

Officer.com — *www.officer.com*
This is a database of links to all kinds of crime and law enforcement sites.

Organized Crime: A Crime Statistics Site — *www.crime.org*
If you need any technical numbers about crime rates in the United States, this is a great source. You always want your script to be as accurate as possible.

Organized Crime Registry — *members.tripod.com/~orgcrime/index.htm*
James Graham maintains a well-organized site that offers articles, news, and FAQs covering not just the American mafia, but the Russian mafia, Japanese yakuza, la cosa nostra, triads, yardies (posses), South American drug cartels, and other crime syndicates.

Cops 'N' Writers: The Definitive Resource for Writers — *www.crime.org*
They are a "consulting service for writers who wish to incorporate law enforcement elements into their writings." An easy-to-use site with lots of information.

CopNet — *www.copnet.org*
CopNet contains a directory to other Web sites and resources in the U.S. organized by state, as well as other countries' justice resources, along with Web sites and other crime links. There's even CopNet radio.

Cops Online — *www.copsonline.com*
This site provides information on police procedure and how-to information for those interested in becoming a cop.

Crime and Clues — *crimeandclues.com*
This excellent resource is edited by Daryl W. Clemens. It has tons of information, from fingerprinting to how to take testimonial evidence — everything you would need to know to make your characters as believable as possible. The most important part of this site is its top-notch breakdown of crime-scene investigation — the protecting, processing, and reconstructing of the scene.

FBI — *www.fbi.gov*
Their Web site offers all kinds of depressing information about wanted criminals and killers, but it also has lots of good data that could be useful to any writer. Of interest, the FBI home page now offers My FBI (*www.fbi.gov/yourfbi.htm*). Here you will find the history and chronology of the FBI, firearms, and:

FBI's Famous Cases —
www.fbi.gov/yourfbi/history/famcases/famcases.htm
Nicely prepared monographs on some of the most notorious criminals in our country's history. Each record includes information and photos on the crimes and investigations.

Drug Enforcement Agency (DEA) — *www.usdoj.gov/dea/*
Their official Web site has some good information.

DNA FORENSICS

Writers working with the mystery or crime genres will more than likely need some information on DNA forensics, especially with today's crime-scene technology.

Yahoo Category: Forensics — *dir.yahoo.com/science/forensics*
Everything you might need to know, from forensic psychology to anthropology.

Human Genome Project DNA Forensics —
www.ornl.gov/hgmis/elsi/forensics.html
This site includes a glossary, acronyms, FAQs, genetics facts, and lots of other useful information.

PATHOLOGY

Pathweb Search Engine — *155.37.5.7/PWINDEX/SearchOptions.cfm*
I was pleasantly surprised when I discovered this site. It is maintained by the Pathology Department at University of Connecticut Health Center. It includes an excellent search interface.

PRIVATE DETECTIVES

In *The Big Sleep* (1946), Humphrey Bogart plays private detective Philip Marlowe. The film, as well as Bogart's performance, set the standard from which all future "private eye" films would be judged. In 1974, Jack Nicholson played L.A. private detective Jake Gittes in Roman Polanski's marvelous realization of Robert Towne's screenplay *Chinatown*. Private eye mysteries, for me at least, make for some of the most interesting stories. In order to write crime or private eye stories today, you'll need to know a lot more about forensics and pathology than did screenwriter

William Faulkner (*The Big Sleep*). There are plenty of online resources to help you discover everything about modern-day private eyes.

Tactics: Private Investigations — *www.tacticsone.com*
This site offers everything you might want to know about private eyes. They even have a book you can purchase that has lots of information in it.

Secrets of Top Private Eyes — *www.howtoinvestigate.com*
There's a book you can buy and a course you can take. They also offer a "members area" on the site that contains an online version of the book. You'll have to pay for access. There are also several free areas that make a trip to this site well worth it.

RELIGION & MYTHS

The Perseus Project — *www.perseus.tufts.edu*
A very impressive collection of information on ancient studies, including a vast amount on religion.

BuddhaNet — *buddhanet.net*
An information network that provides articles and information about Buddhist history and culture.

Hindu Resources Online — *www.hindu.org*
Links to Hindu organizations, leaders, and resources worldwide.

Islam.com — *www.islam.com*
It's the Yahoo of Islamic Web sites, with links organized nicely in a directory listing all facets of Islamic history and information.

Vatican: The Holy See — *www.vatican.va*
Their official Web site consists of news, columns, and a nice archive. It can be accessed in a variety of languages.

4Mythology.com — *4mythology.com*
The 4Anything Network has a lot of very useful Web sites covering a wide spectrum of topics and categories. This particular site covers mythology from virtually every part of the world and throughout history, including Greek, Roman, Egyptian, and Norse mythology, and much more.

SERIAL KILLERS

If you want a few great examples of what a good serial killer movie is supposed to look like, check out *Manhunter*, *Silence of the Lambs*, and *Se7en*. All three films had one very important element going for them: a masterful screenplay. Screenwriters Michael Mann (*Manhunter*), Ted Tally (*Silence of the Lambs*), and Andrew Kevin Walker (*Se7en*) were able to weave complex story lines with technical elements in a flawless manner. When you sit down to write one of these kinds of scripts, you'll need to know not only things about serial killers, but law-enforcement and crime-scene professionals. From the technical language used by officials to characteristics and traits of serial killers, it's very important you do your research well.

Guest book for Serial Killers — *www.tdl.com/~kitty/guestbook.html*
This site needs to be taken with a grain of salt, and then some. But make no mistake, it will give you goose bumps, and sometimes the posts I've read are just plain disturbing. You see, some of the participants claim to be actual serial killers. Here's an example of one post from someone claiming to be a serial killer (warning: this is disturbing):

"Good evening or morning in some cases. This is an interesting site but a lot of these people are quite sad... I myself have killed on three occasions (not kidding) and feel that these people could use a real insight from an active serial killer and not some want-to-be psychopath who dreams of slaughtering his/her teachers and class mates. The act of killing is intense beyond intense. Far greater than a sex act. It is owning the person and playing God. Having domination deciding to kill or allow mercy.... it is extremely powerful. My murder method is interesting, not original but interesting. I lure the victim to my home where I act all nice and humane and suddenly I pounce. Instead of the usual stabbing or bludgeoning I drown the victim in the bath whilst they are still awake. The fact that they struggle and their struggles become weaker is a major thrill. The moment is all that matters to people of my ilk."

Another warning: If you decide to contact someone who is claiming to be a serial killer, do so at your own risk.

The Crime Web: Serial Killer News — *www.crimeweb.homestead.com*
This site is well maintained, very professional, and represents a collection of photos and other information about serial killers. It features a historical calendar of events charting the careers of famous serial killers. If you're writing about serial killers, you should know about something called the *serial killer signature*: "The killer's signature is the killer's calling card, what makes his crime unique even if he consciously changes the MO or any other facet of the killings." There is also a links section to other Web sites dedicated to serial killers.

The Serial Killer Hit List — *www.mayhem.net/Crime/serial1.html*
This site is almost too well maintained for my taste. But it is an excellent resource for common-sense information and facts on America's worst serial killers. From the Web site:

"Serial killers tend to be white, heterosexual males in their twenties and thirties who are sexually dysfunctional and have low self-esteem. Their methodical rampages are almost always sexual in nature. Their killings are usually part of an elaborate fantasy that builds to a climax at the moment of their murderous outburst. Serial killers generally murder strangers with cooling off periods between each crime. Many enjoy cannibalism, necrophilia, and keep trophy-like body parts as mementos of their work. Serial killers are sadistic in nature. Some return to crime scenes or grave sites of their victims to fantasize about their deeds. Many like to insert

28

themselves in the investigation of their crimes and some enjoy taunting authorities with letters or carefully placed pieces of evidence."

SPECIAL OPS

Special Ops — *www.specialoperations.com*
Easily the most comprehensive military and civilian special operations and counter-terrorism site on the Web. You can conduct research from their site, request information, or just ask a question. They also have books and other material for sale.

SLANG

Aussie Slang — *www.geocities.com/Heartland/Plains/9740/slang.html*
Need that character to sound just like Russell Crowe? No problem: There is a resource online called Aussie Slang. But remember, do not overdo it when writing slang. Here's an example of what not to do: "Deh f-ucking guy talks-a like-a this-a." You should only have to use a few words to get the sound effect across. Just make your characters sound natural.

Gangster Slang — *www.swingordie.com/slang/gslang.html*
From the site: "You dumb mug, get your mitts off the marbles before I stuff that mud-pipe down your mush." Not a bad example if your script is set in the 1940s.

Twists, Slugs, and Roscoes: A Glossary of Hardboiled Slang — *www.miskatonic.org/slang.html*
A fun-to-read site with lots of cool and funny slang for the hard-boiled detective story you might be writing.

Cool Jargon of the Day — *www.jargon.net*
If you feel you need to be hip and on the cutting edge of what kind of language young people use today, this is a nice resource.

Yahoo Slang Listing — *dir.yahoo.com/reference/dictionaries/slang/*
Once again, Yahoo is just a great resource for these types of listings.

Dictionary of Street Drug Slang —
www.drugs.indiana.edu/slang/home.html
This dictionary contains more than 3,000 street-drug slang terms and more than 1,200 additions from the National Drug and Crime Clearinghouse slang list.

TECHNOSPEAK

Hacker Speech Style —
www.eps.mcgill.ca/jargon/html/hacker-speech-style.html
Need that computer geek in your script to sound like a real hacker and not some contrived Hollywood stereotype? This is your place.

FINDING AN EXPERT

Yahoo! Experts — *experts.yahoo.com*
What would we do without Yahoo? You can post questions, get answers, or you can just browse the listings. No matter how obscure, you can almost always find an expert in virtually any subject.

Refdesk.com — *www.refdesk.com/expert.html*
Ask the experts at *refdesk.com*. Need to find an expert on diamonds so you can incorporate that into your screenplay? No problem. I found Ask about Diamonds (*www.vandaaz.com/ASK.HTML*) at *refdesk.com*. There

seem to be a few topics that weren't covered in Yahoo that you might find here. Refdesk offers links to a couple hundred expert centers, making them another great option.

Answers.com — *www.answers.com*
You've got questions, and they've got answers. This is a nice site with one of the better Web designs around. *Answers.com* was founded by idealab! in 1996 to provide real-time, expert answers to consumer questions on any topic.

HISTORICAL RESEARCH

Period screenplays are a hard sell. However, after the success of James Cameron's 1997 hit *Titanic*, several more blockbuster films quickly followed, including *Saving Private Ryan*, *The Thin Red Line*, *Gladiator*, and *The Patriot* — not to mention this year's box office hit, *Pearl Harbor*. There are also countless projects in development, such as *Alexander the Great*, *King Arthur*, and several more war stories, including one based on the best-selling book, *We Were Soldiers Once… and Young*, by Gen. Harold G. Moore and Joseph L. Galloway.

For example, let's say you're writing about the 1960s. You'll need to know the language they used, the makes and models of popular cars, clothing, and don't forget about the major political and social issues of the time. There are things that could pop in and out of discussions between your characters, like political and religious issues or leaders. Sometimes, because of hindsight, you can even find some nice humor to weave into your story or dialogue. So get it right, and have some fun.

About American History — *americanhistory.about.com*
Just an incredible online resource. If you're writing about any topic in American history, this should be one of your first stops on the Web.

Document Center —
www.lib.umicb.edu/libhome/Documents.center/index.html
The University of Michigan offers a detailed archive of historical and current federal, local, and international papers.

WWW Virtual Library —
history.cc.ukans.edu/history/WWW_history_main.html
Extensive links to sites on medieval, ancient, Roman, and African history as well as Asian studies, Egyptology, and more. They even have a discussion list, which might be a good place to start your research with a question.

AMDOCS — *www.ukans.edu/carrie/docs/amdocs_index.html*
With documents for the study of American history starting in 1492, this site is geared more towards scholarly research, but you might want to immerse yourself in the period you're writing about by getting to know it in depth.

History Cooperative — *www.historycooperative.org*
Research can be accomplished with their searchable journals and articles archive.

Historical research should not be limited just to textbooks. If you can, find survivors, witnesses, experts, and anyone else who has firsthand knowledge of the events or time period you are writing about. The Internet is also a great way to search out those people, using some of the resources I've discussed in this chapter. Don't limit yourself just to the Internet; go out and talk to people.

CHAPTER THREE

SCREENWRITING RESOURCES

You can learn online everything you need to know to start writing screenplays. That's not to say that the Web should be a substitute for some of the excellent books out there, because it's not. But make no mistake, whether you're a monetarily challenged writer or have cash to spend, the Web has plenty to offer.

The biggest complaint I have about the Web is the amount of poor (and flat-out bad) information that exists. That's one of the reasons why I wrote this book. The resources I'll be pointing out have something to offer.

By no means can I cover every Web resource available in one chapter or one book. There are simply too many of them. It is my intention to guide you to a few select places where you can increase your knowledge of screenwriting. From any one of these selections, you may very well go off in a new direction — you know, like a plot point. I don't mind what direction you go in, just as long as you go.

IN CYBERSPACE, NO ONE CAN HEAR YOU SCREAM

Sometimes I just want to scream when I am online. It might be a slow connection speed or a slow Web site, or I'm just not finding good information. The degree of varying opinions to be found can cause frustration as well. There are a lot of self-proclaimed experts out there, so be careful whose advice you take, as anyone can start a site and write whatever they want. Most important, you do not have to follow any one person's advice verbatim, including mine. Pick and choose what works best for you, and put it all together to develop your own unique style.

FROM "HYPER-DRAMAS" TO HOME PAGES

Charles Deemer is *the* pioneer for screenwriters on the Web. He was the first to establish a screenwriting site, and he is one of the most well-known online screenwriting personalities. His classes and books have helped thousands of writers, including me.

In 1994, Deemer founded the Web's first site for screenwriters, The Screenwriters & Playwrights Home Page.[1] Today, there are thousands of home pages and Web sites that deal with screenwriting in one form or another.

As an enthusiast of "hyper-dramas" (dramatic scripts written with simulta-neous, multiple lines of action), Deemer became the founder of the first screenwriting Web site almost by accident. "My motive for starting a Web site," explains Deemer, "was to teach myself HTML."[2]

After learning the skill by creating a personal home page, he set out to make a Web site for playwrights and screenwriters. "There was nothing online for playwrights or screenwriters, so that's why I did the site," adds Deemer. He wanted to fill a need or, as he says, "a vacuum" — and just how big a vacuum, no one could have predicted.

THE BEGINNER

You've never written a screenplay before, have no idea how to start writing one, and probably need help with proper screenplay format and other basics. If this in any way describes you, then you're a beginner. At this stage it's important to read as much as possible. This should include produced screenplays, articles, books, and interviews.

READ PRODUCED SCREENPLAYS

Read the scripts from some of your favorite movies. Just be careful, as

---

[1] *www.teleport.com/~cdeemer/scrwriter.html*
[2] Hypertext Markup Language, better known as HTML, is what Web Masters use to post text and other information on Web pages to be viewed in your browser.

34

some of the material you'll see online will be production drafts that include camera directions.[3] You will avoid using such directions when you write.

iScriptdb — *www.iscriptdb.com*
This is a searchable database of produced screenplays on the Web — over 500 listed at the time of this writing — and an excellent resource to help you find the script you want fast. You can even browse it by screenwriter or by title.

Drew's Script-O-Rama — *www.script-o-rama.com*
The original online source for scripts. Over the past few years, his site has been behind in updating its links. However, one of the great things about Drew's site is his dedication to the unproduced writer. He will post your script on his site if you think that will help you. (For more information on posting your screenplay online, see Chapter Nine.)

Movie-Page — *www.movie-page.com*
One of the best-kept secrets on the Web, their movie script archive is constantly updated and always well maintained. They also offer movie reviews, DVD reviews, and news.

Joblo's Movie Emporium — *www.joblo.com*
A fun site with more than just screenplays to browse through. Joblo also offers movie news, reviews, trailers, and much more.

BEFORE YOU START

So you wanna be a screenwriter? What does it take, and what can you expect as you head down that path? For one, I think it's important for you to know that the "overnight" success stories you sometimes hear

---

[3] Do not direct the directors in your script. Such camera directions are things like: CLOSE UP, DISSOLVE, SERIES OF SHOTS, ANGLE ON, PAN, and others.

about are so few and far between that you would be wise to dismiss that thought from your head. My advice is to prepare yourself mentally for the long haul. There are also a lot of other things you should know. You need honest and straightforward advice.

So you Wanna be a Screenwriter? — *home.earthlink.net/~scribbler/wannabe.html*
&
Before you Begin — *home.earthlink.net/~scribbler/facts.html*
Professional screenwriter Brad Mirman (*Knight Moves*) has some important and interesting advice before you set out to make your first million-dollar spec sale. There are several columns here that you should read. Mirman has had a presence on the Web for years. His site is no longer updated, but who can blame him. I think it's cool that he even tries to give back to the aspiring screenwriter.

Is Screenwriting Right For You? — *www.cyberfilmschool.com/columns/deemer_1.htm*
Charles Deemer, author of *Screenwright: The Craft of Screenwriting*, is an experienced and well-respected writer. His site, mentioned earlier, is a great resource for information on how to write your screenplay.

"Hollyweird" — *www.screenwritersutopia.com/pros/nba.html*
I call Bud Fleisher the working man's screenwriter because the guy has written a ton of scripts and has over a dozen credits to his name. Yet, you've probably never heard of him. Bud's "Hollyweird" column cuts to the chase and avoids all the b.s. It's the honest truth from his perspective. If you read his columns carefully, you'll learn something new each time about the bottomless pit that some believe Hollywood really is.

The Hollywood Writer — *www.io.com/~dbrown/index.html*
A poignant and honest presentation on the realities of moving to Hollywood in search of fame and fortune as a "Hollywood writer." For right now, don't worry about moving to Hollywood. You need to get started first. If the time comes when you're ready to take the leap, then consider all of your options.

SELECT INTERVIEWS FOR BEGINNERS

You can learn a lot by paying close attention to what the pros have to say about the craft of screenwriting. I really believe you can never read too many interviews as long as they are conducted with experienced pros.

Interview with Chris Vogler —
www.absolutewrite.com/screenwriting/chris_vogler.htm
Jenna Glatzer, from her *absolutewrite.com* Web site, conducts an informative and inspirational interview with the author of *The Writer's Journey: Mythic Structure for Writers*, Chris Vogler.

Interview Excerpt — Vogler on the most common mistakes new writers make: "Overexplaining and overwriting. They give a lot of unnecessary detail because they are afraid their audience — the readers of the script — won't get it. We get it. Give your readers credit and let them participate. It's amazing what you can leave out and still achieve full communication."

Writing the Picture: An Interview with Robin Russin and William Missouri Downs —
www.screenwritersutopia.com/interviews/wtp-kenna.html
Kenna McHugh offers a noteworthy interview with Robin Russin and William Missouri, the authors of *Screenplay: Writing the Picture*. This interview is really a must for the intermediate screenwriter as well. It contains information on what makes good screenwriting, advice on pitching your screenplay, and much more.

Interview Excerpt — Robin Russin on the dangers of writing for free: "There are several dangers. First and foremost, you risk wasting months of your life on projects that aren't going to happen. Hollywood is full of hustlers, people trying to be producers, and very few of them will succeed. But all of them are happy to waste your time if there's no downside, no cost to them. It's generally true that if someone is for real in this business, and if they value your work, they will both have the money and be willing to spend it to acquire your work or services. If they're not willing to pay you, then you know that either they're not really in a position to get something made, or they don't really consider your work worth the money, in which case they're not going to put much of their time or capital into seeing it made into a film."

Interview with Richard Krevolin —
www.screenwritersutopia.com/interviews/richard.html
Richard Krevolin's book *Screenwriting From The Soul* is one of the most inspirational books on screenwriting that I've ever read. I was fortunate enough to interview him.

Interview Excerpt — Richard Krevolin on what makes good screenwriting: "When you can tell the writer cares; when language is still important; when the formulas are all toyed with to the point that unexpected things happen; when audiences are treated like intelligent adults and their emotions are touched. Touch me and I'll care....And in the end, it is a visceral not a cerebral medium, so it is about heart and soul, not mind...."

Michael Hauge Interview —
www.screenwritersutopia.com/interviews/99_hauge.html
Michael Hauge's award-winning book, *Writing Screenplays That Sell*, should be part of your personal library. He is a script consultant, story editor, writer, and independent producer who has made his living in the Hollywood film and television industries since the mid-seventies. This is an excellent interview that every aspiring screenwriter should read. Pay particular attention to his comments on theme and character growth.

WRITING YOUR SCRIPT

It's not enough to have a desire to write, and it's not enough to want to write like your favorite professional screenwriter. You'll find it's pretty hard facing a blank computer screen for the first time. Whenever you sit down to write, there is potential for short-term writer's block, hesitation, or lack of confidence in what you're about to put down. With this in mind, you should at least have a good idea of what a screenplay is supposed to look like, what it is supposed to accomplish, and how to execute it properly. To put it simply, a screenplay is a blueprint for a movie. Here are some more basics you should know.

THE BASICS

As a teacher, consultant, script reviewer, and judge for the Screenwriting Showcase Awards, I can't help but get discouraged whenever I see a screenplay that is improperly formatted and/or unbound. It is reprehensible. It does not deserve to be read and usually will not be read. Send an unbound screenplay to an agency, and they'll throw it in the recycling bin without reading it. Contests have more of an obligation to read your script, but that very crucial first impression is a wash. You've worked long and hard on the damn thing; do not get lazy in the end. And remember, the greatest screenplay in the world is rendered useless when it is not read.

YOUR COVER

Your script should have a cover. Avoid flashy colors. Use a heavy-stock paper. On it should be the title and your name, centered.

Script Title
By: Your Name

"A JOHN CARPENTER FILM"

As I write this, the Directors Guild of America (DGA) and the Writers Guild of America (WGA) are in a heated battle over possessory credits, where the director places "A film by" credit on the project — as if he or she were the only driving force behind the movie. You can imagine how the screenwriter, producers, and actors feel about such pretentiousness. It's not necessary to announce your work or yourself. "A screenplay by" statement only makes you look like an amateur. It will be obvious that you're a screenwriter, and it will be very apparent that you've written a screenplay. Leave the announcements to the directors.

CONTACT INFORMATION

In the lower right-hand corner of the cover, or on the second page, should be your contact information. If you have an agent, that information should be listed. Your social security number is not needed. Giving it out in today's age of technology and computer hacking is dangerous. I can't think of one solid reason why anyone would need it just to read your screenplay.

COPYRIGHT & REGISTRATION

For information on how to copyright your material, see Chapter Nine. Including a copyright and/or registration number on your script cover is not necessary. Place it on a second page along with your contact information. Do not place the date of copyright or registration on the script. If the first thing a producer or agent sees is a script that was copyrighted three years ago, they'll obviously view the material as "old." They like material to be "fresh."

The cover is attached to the script with two brass brads (see below).

YOUR PAGES

Each page must have the same margins: 1.5 inches left, which is necessary to account for the three-hole punch, and 1.0 inch right. Each page of your screenplay must have three holes on the left-hand edge. In the top and bottom holes must be a brass brad. To review: three-hole punch, top and bottom brass brads. (Note: if you are using a screenwriting program, the margins are taken care of for you.)

Do not use fancy fonts that are hard to read. You should use Courier 12.

YOUR PAPER

Standard multi-use paper is fine: 20 lb. 8½ by 11 inches. Use only white paper.

YOUR WRITING

Screenwriting has been called an art, a craft, and even a science. A screenplay has a unique format and, depending on whom you ask, a consistent formula. As far as who is right or wrong, I'll leave that up to the experts. But I will tell you this: If the story you're writing does not have a clear beginning, middle, and end, its chances of selling drop significantly. And with that in mind, just because your story is structured correctly, and has all the elements that make a successful screenplay, it still may not sell.

When it comes down to it, screenwriting, like anything else, is really about ability and talent. You either got it or you don't, kid. Is your writing good enough to hold your reader's attention? Is your prose engaging, entertaining, or witty when required? Do you have a knack for knowing when less is more, when to get into a scene at the right time, and when to get out of it? Do you have that kind of ability in you? Only time will tell. You must hone and develop your skill, and it could take years to perfect.

If the written and unwritten rules of the screenwriting profession are followed, I truly believe the cream always rises to the top. You will get your chance, if you have the ability and the talent. A few years ago, that wasn't always the case. Even today with the Internet, people will still argue that new writers are not getting a fair chance. Keep your state of mind positive. Learn the basics, and keep writing.

SCREENPLAY FORMAT

If you're a visual person like me, then all you will need to do is review a couple of samples of screenplay format and away you'll go. However, what can make things a tad confusing is that every presentation seems to offer subtle differences in proper screenplay format. My advice is just to pay attention to the big picture, and don't let all of the divergent opinions stop you from writing.

FORMAT EXAMPLE

Each scene is made up of a Scene Heading, Description, Characters, Dialogue and Action lines. These are the basics. There are other things that I will not go into, but you are sure to encounter them as you do your homework.

Scene Heading (also known as a Slugline)

```
INT. HALLWAY - NIGHT
```

Notice it is all in caps. Use INT. for inside and EXT. for outside. Tell us where we are, and follow that up by telling us if it is DAY or NIGHT.

Description

Underneath the scene heading is a description of the area. What is important about where we are? Who's there? Try not to ramble on. Give us just enough to get a few snapshots of the important details.

Characters

```
                CHARACTER NAME
```

This is always in caps and always centered.

Dialogue

What the character has to say. Try to keep it real, and avoid large chunks of dialogue in your screenplay.

Action lines

What is the character doing? What is happening?

And now, the scene. Try to identify what we just talked about. Each element is represented.

```
INT. HALLWAY - NIGHT

Dimly lit, drab, and old.  The wood floor creeks as Frank
makes his way, slowly, with gun drawn.

There's a blood-splatter on the wall, Frank gives it a
quick look.  It's fresh, but where's the body?

Blood droppings on the floor lead him to a door; it's
half-open.  More blood.  Frank, against the wall now,
slides up to the door, gun ready.

                        FRANK
                Who's in there? Are you hurt
                bad? Talk to me.

He checks quickly behind him.  He's nervous.  Frank then
makes a move and enters the apartment, gun raised.
```

This is a very basic presentation. I urge you to read a few of the more in-depth presentations I have listed below. If you ever have a question, do not hesitate to contact the author of each article. You can usually find an e-mail address or some other contact information on each page.

How to Format a Script —
www.screenstyle.com/screenstyle/howtoforscre.html

A great overview of the basics of script formatting from *screenstyle.com* — one of the best I have found. The first lesson is, "There is no 100% absolutely correct way to format a script!" And it's true, so focus on the very basics.

Nicholl Fellowship's Formatting Sample —
www.oscars.org/nicholl/format_a.txt
A nice page showing proper screenplay format by Ann Garretson from The Nicholl Fellowship Web site.

Screenplay Format — *www.screenwritersworkshop.com/format.html*
The Screenwriters Workshop offers a short and concise primer on proper screenplay format. Very useful!

SCREENWRiT Script Format —
www.panam.edu/scrnwrit/chap12.html
A popular FAQ for screenwriters, and rightfully so; it's an excellent presentation covering everything from your cover to the text inside.

Screenplay Formatting — *www.dclough.dircon.co.uk/SW_Form.htm*
A little on the short side, but worth a read.

SCREENWRITING TERMINOLOGY

From the time you write *Fade In*, to the end and *Fade Out*, there are some terms you should be aware of, especially since you'll be using some of them quite often. (See also the glossary of terms at the back of this book.)

Glossary of Screenwriting Terms —
www.screenwritersutopia.com/basicterms.html
A complete list of terms and usage that every aspiring screenwriter should know.

SCREENPLAY STRUCTURE

The three-act structure — beginning (setup), middle (development), and end (resolution) — is very simple and yet very important. Don't jump around in your story. Use a clearly developed three-act structure to support your story. Don't leave any loose ends, leave nothing unresolved when you type *Fade Out*. Don't get hung up on plot points and stuff like that yet. Right now just make sure you have an idea of how to develop your story so it is readable. As you gain confidence, you can start taking chances and writing more like Scott Frank (*Out of Sight*) or Christopher Noland (*Memento*). For now, stay focused on learning the craft.

Dramatic Structure — *www.teleport.com/~cdeemer/Structure.html*
Another excellent offering by Charles Deemer. Pay particular attention to his short presentation of Syd Field's Paradigm at the bottom of the page.

Introducing Structure — *www.dclough.dircon.co.uk/SW_Stc1.htm*
This is excellent. You might just want to read this and move on to another topic. It's very short, but to the point and informative. From the page: "If a script is going well, you may never need to think about structure at all. Sometimes the gods make you such presents: a story that literally writes itself. In such circumstances, you usually know instinctively the best and most effective choices to make."

Screenplay Structure —
www.netxweb.com/screenplays/pages/structure.htm
Ignore the author's page breakdown; nothing has to happen by a certain page. That's not structure; that's a formula. The author does present some points worth noting, but once again be careful with this "formula" presentation.

OUTLINING

Before you begin writing, you may want to consider outlining your story. Not everyone does; it's up to the individual writer. Do what works best for you. Here is an excellent guide from The Screenwriters Workshop:

The Step-Outline: Getting to the Bare Bones of Your Idea —
www.screenwritersworkshop.com/step_outline.html
Writing "from the inside out," as Robert McKee (*Story: Substance, Structure, Style, and the Principles of Screenwriting*) suggests, requires that you first start developing your story using a step-outline. Consult this excellent resource for more on the "inside out" approach to using outlines.

THE INTERMEDIATE SCREENWRITER

"Screenwriting is a craft that occasionally rises to the level of an art. An art because there are times when it taps directly into the human heart, transcending time, place, language and culture. A craft because it depends upon form, concept, character and structure."

— Syd Field

Perhaps you're not new to screenwriting. Maybe you've just finished your first script or have several completed. You're just starting to find yourself as a writer. If this describes you, then you're most likely in the intermediate stage. This is where you grow and blossom as a writer. You still need to keep reading and, most important, keep writing as much as possible. But get comfortable; you could be here awhile.

LEARNING THE CRAFT

Screenwriting is first and foremost about structure, as far as I am concerned. Once you have a strong grasp for the structure, you can better develop your skill as a writer. A good screenplay should have a solid story line (spine) to hold it together. Your characters should be well developed, have clear arcs, and travel through your story with a clear dramatic need.

The Screenwriting Craft — *www.screenwritersutopia.com/rebelrp.html* This tutorial is well known on the Web. You can find it on several sites, and in my opinion it's one of the best resources available. Writer/producer Alex Epstein offers up a superb page that acts more like a self-help course on screenwriting, covering everything from formatting to character development and structure. I've read books that were not as well thought-out and presented as Epstein's presentation here.

Screenwriting Tips — *www.vcu.edu/artweb/playwriting/screentips.html* Intended as a tip sheet for playwrights interested in writing a screenplay, by Richard Toscan, it's one of the better presentations I have found online.

JOIN A SCREENWRITING GROUP

Down the road, this could be one of the most important things you do. The friendships and camaraderie you build will become a source of strength. The Web can be a lonely and cold place without some online group or area where you feel comfortable asking questions and venting a little.

Screenwriters' Newsgroup — *news:misc.writing.screenplays*
The Usenet screenwriters' list is usually a great place to debate important issues and just hang out. There are professionals who post and interact. As you do not have to use your real name or a real e-mail address, it's hard to tell who's responding to whom. As of late, the newsgroup has really become a stalking ground for flame wars and other nonsense, so be careful and check your feelings at the door.

Screenwriters' Internetwork —
www.geocities.com/devote_72/screenwriters-internetwork/network.html
This site offers many different groups, and most are open for serious and enlightening discussion. I highly recommend this to the serious screenwriter. There is a Screenwriters Support Group, which is also a great place to find friendship and, of course, positive support.

Yahoo Groups: Screenwriting —
dir.groups.yahoo.com/dir/Entertainment___Arts/Movies/Filmmaking /Screenwriting
Here you'll find dozens of groups totaling thousands of members. The best ones are very active. I recommend Margo Prescott's Screenwriting Group, and HollyScript by the *Hollywood Scriptwriter*. You will need to register — and in some cases apply — to join the group.

Utopia Word Play: The Screenwriters Chat Room —
www.screenwritersutopia.com/chat.html
A Java chat room that does not require any special membership to access and is very easy to use. It tends to be more active at night, when there always seems to be a friendly crowd.

120pages2go — *www.egroups.com/group/120pages2go*
This group is for beginners and offers a friendly environment. There are a couple of advanced writers who answer questions and share knowledge.

Mark's Screenwriting Chat —
www.geocities.com/Hollywood/Theater/6448/message.html
Usually every Tuesday night from 8:00 p.m. to 9:00 p.m. (CST), there
are lively, yet friendly, chat sessions taking place.

WordPlay Forums —
www.wordplayer.com/forums/welcome.html
This is one of the most active boards and is always friendly. There are
two boards, "Movies" and "Scripts," and both are excellent. The moder-
ator does a great job of watching over the board. There are also several
professional writers who post regularly.

MORE ON SCREENPLAY STRUCTURE

Here are some more refined and in-depth approaches to screenplay
structure. These are intended for the more advanced screenwriter who
is less likely to become confused by some of these divergent presentations.

The Need for Structure, Part 1 —
www.beckerfilms.com/structure.html
Independent filmmaker Josh Becker presents a charming view of structure, or as he would put it, the lack of structure these days.

Why Screenplay Structure? —
www.brainlink.com/~zahir13/structure.html
This presentation demonstrates the classic three-act structure using a
screenplay sample provided by the author.

David Siegel's Two-goal Nine-act Paradigm —
www.dsiegel.com/film/Film_home.html
Seigel's nine-act structure is essentially a refined look at the three-act
structure.

49

Plot Devices — *www.wordplayer.com/columns/wp32.Plot.Devices.html*
Professional screenwriters Terry Rossio and Ted Elliot (*Shrek*, *Aladdin*) have one of the best sites on the Internet for aspiring and advanced screenwriters. They donate their time freely and interact often. This particular column is an excellent presentation on screenwriting (I thought placing it here was most appropriate). From the column: "Gathered here are a whole bunch of our concepts and devices and ideas we've come up with over the years."

A Brief History of Hollywood Dramaturgy and Modern Screenplay Structure: A Journey Over Time and Borders — *geocities.com/Hollywood/Academy/5698/adramaturgy.html*
Mikael Colville-Andersen presents an interesting take on structure and its origins. From the site: "The dramaturgical structure inherent in most Hollywood films was fine-tuned over the years until reaching the point at which we now find ourselves: the three-act structure, the plot points, the time frame and such-like pandemonium."

The Three-Act Structure

The Importance of Three-Act Storytelling — *www.cyberfilmschool.com/columns/deemer_2.htm*
Charles Deemer's article via the Cyber Film School is a breezy and consuming offering on the importance of understanding screenplay structure. He efficiently covers such topics as dramatic movement, goals, and conflict — and how these work within the three-act structure.

Act Structure Demystified, Part I — *screenwriting.about.com/arts/screenwriting/library/weekly/aa052598.htm*
I'm a big fan of this site and the work Allen White has put into it. This is Part One in a nice breakdown of the three-act structure. The series offers examples from some of our favorite movies.[4]

---

[4] As of this writing I was informed that Allen White was leaving as editor of this Web site.

Story Line

Advancing A Complex Plot Along a Story Line: A Review of *L.A. Confidential* — *www.teleport.com/~bjscript/storyispromise.htm*
Bill Johnson, author of *The Story is a Promise*, discusses his paradigm for developing a new sense of clarity concerning the elements of a story and how they work together within the framework of the story line.

CHARACTER DEVELOPMENT

Developing good characters in your story is hard to do, but it is essential. Having weak characters means a weak story. Your goal is to give your story at least one strong character with a clear dramatic need (what it is they want or must accomplish). Every one of your main characters should have a true and consistent voice. Remember that your characters should be like real people with flaws and weaknesses, which will make them more compelling and interesting. For more on character development try the following:

Establishing the Point of View —
www.hollywoodnetwork.com/hn/writing/swls/columns/pov.html
A great piece written by author Linda Seger (*Making A Good Script Great*). When developing your story and your characters, you need to decide whose story it is. From whose point of view (POV) is the story being told? This is important. Think of the movie *The Silence of the Lambs*. Whose story was it? We saw everything through Clarice's eyes and from her perspective. Not every story is going to have a dominant POV. It all depends on the characters and kind of story you're writing.

Pushing Our Characters to the Limit —
www.singlelane.com/escript/post2.htm#dw
Diana Wagman has done an excellent job with this short and concise presentation. This is part of an introduction for the Screenwriting

Workshop at E-script. From her opening statement: "character being the single most important element in a screenplay," it therefore must be developed carefully.

Impressive Failure —
www.wordplayer.com/columns/wp08.Impressive.Failure.html
From the Wordplay site professional screenwriter Terry Rossio discusses some of our favorite movie characters including Indiana Jones and others. From the column: "The actions and decisions of the characters are what create the basic situations of the story. Those key moments are where the plot really happens."

Character Development — *www.dclough.dircon.co.uk/SW_Chr1.htm*
From the page: "Decisions you make about characters may be instinctive but they should never be arbitrary. Remember, character (in the abstract) is the engine that drives your story; characters (in the specific) are the colliding atoms that give substance to the world of your creation."

The Core of Character — *www.wga.org/craft/character.html*
This site is compiled and edited by Hillary Atkin, who interviews several professional writers about the importance of developing good characters.

Taking Characters Seriously —
www.vcu.edu/artweb/playwriting/characterdev.html
The content on this site is from *The Playwriting Seminars: The Full-Length Play*. Essentially, they want you to take your characters seriously, let them into your head, and get to know them. Good advice, and a nice essay with some useful information.

The Character Problem — *www.nyscreenwriter.com/article34.htm*
"What makes characters interesting and appealing?" By avoiding standard formulas, you make your characters more interesting. Don't be afraid to make them flawed! This great article is brought to you by the *New York Screenwriter*.

Cast Yourself a Superstar — *www.teleport.com/~cdeemer/tip13.ram*
Charles Deemer has a great RealAudio series offering all kinds of advice.
Here's one of the better offerings. Check out this excellent presentation
on character development.

Creating Dynamic Characters — *hollywoodnet.com/Johnson/wchar.htm*
Bill Johnson offers a series of columns on the Hollywood Network covering
screenwriting structure and character development.

Creating Characters by About.com —
screenwriting.about.com/arts/screenwriting/library/weekly/aa013099.htm
This is another solid presentation by Allen White concerning how to
develop your characters, how to develop dimensional characters of depth,
how to utilize contradiction when developing your characters, the role of
conflict, and much more.

The Hero

Importance of "The Hero" — *www.teleport.com/~cdeemer/hero.html*
From the site: "A producer, who chooses to remain anonymous, emphasizes
the importance of a clear hero who moves the plot." Includes a short note
on the "structural track" of the main character.

A Cure for the Passive Protagonist —
www.writersconsortium.com/pages/writingtips.htm#ACurefor
thePassiveProtagonist
A trap that some beginning writers succumb to is the "passive" hero, or
protagonist. Your hero must be active and always moving or developing.

Example of the Jarvis Method, using *Star Wars* —
www.screenwritersutopia.com/interviews/~jarvis.htm
John Jarvis is the creator of *The Jarvis Method* of storytelling. Mr. Jarvis
discusses the theme hero and the action hero, among other archetypes,
and how they relate and differ.

The Antagonist

Welcome to the Dark Side —
www.wga.org/WrittenBy/1997/0297/villains.html
From *Written By* magazine on the WGA site comes an article by Zorianna Kit about developing the villain character.

My Mother the Antagonist —
www.scriptsecrets.com/articles/antagon.htm
Professional screenwriter and author of *The Secrets of Action Screenwriting*, William C. Martell, offers up an excellent article on what makes a laudable antagonist. From the page: "Your antagonist creates the conflict in your script, and that conflict has to be something strong enough to carry your story for 110 pages. Something that can go the distance. So your antagonist has to create a problem so big that it will take the whole film for your protagonist to solve it."

DIALOGUE

If William Goldman is to be believed, then dialogue should be the last thing that a fledgling screenwriter would want to worry about. According to Goldman, "[Dialogue]… is among the least important parts of a screenplay." Well, don't believe it for a second! Dialogue is very important, especially when accomplished well. Do avoid talky characters and the overuse of dialogue. Always try to *show* us as opposed to *telling* us how a character is feeling. A great script consists of good, solid dialogue, and sometimes, as Arnold Schwarzenegger would say, "one-liners."

The Dialogue of Eszterhas, Darabont, and Tarantino —
www.screenwritersutopia.com/actionwriter/dialog.html
Three masters of storytelling and, not surprisingly, of dialogue as well, share their thoughts. Making your characters sound real is hard; it takes time to master. Tarantino uses dialogue extremely well. Characters can reveal themselves by which words they use and how they use them.

Writing Effective Dialogue —
screenwriting.about.com/arts/screenwriting/library/weekly/aa080498.htm
What makes dialogue great? This is a very simple and important question raised in the article, which the author then sets out to answer. By taking the time to explain the proper uses of dialogue, this piece separates itself from others. If there is a finer presentation of dialogue usage on the Web, I've failed to find it.

STORYTELLING

Screenwriting, like any kind of dramatic writing, is about storytelling. Beginning with caveman drawings, people have always had the need to pass on knowledge and events with story. Here are some essays and articles on the art of storytelling.

Understanding What A Story Is —
www.teleport.com/~bjscript/wstoryis.htm
Writer Bill Johnson sets out to answer the question, "What is a story?" How to properly go about engaging your audience, how to make a story fulfilling, and the importance of the story's plot in holding everything together.

The Foundation of All Screenwriting — *screenwriters.com/Hauge/*
Michael Hauge's book, *Writing Screenplays That Sell*, is one of the most highly regarded screenwriting publications around. Via the Hollywood Network, he offers a series of columns to help you, from "Creating Powerful Opening Scenes" to "The Rules of Screenwriting."

HIGH CONCEPT

You've probably heard the statement, "*Die Hard* on a bus," or a plane or train. When something is "high-concept," it is easily understood. Some executives say they can see the movie in their head. It doesn't need a lot of explaining. You can picture the movie with one or two sentences of information. Though it is a term that is not as widely used as it once was, the idea behind it will always be important to Hollywood. You would be wise to understand fully what is meant by it.

The Idea is King — *hollywoodnet.com/Trottier/idea.html*
When it comes down to it, the foundation of a salable screenplay is the marketability of the idea that drives it. You need a clear concept, a *high-concept* idea. This excellent column is by author David Trottier (*The Screenwriter's Bible*).

High Concept — *www.teleport.com/~cdeemer/high-concept.html*
How would you define the term *high concept*? Charles Deemer, with the help of others, presents a nice collaboration in defining what it is and how it works.

WRITING FOR LOW-BUDGET FILMS

On the other end of the spectrum are stories that are developed for their artistic nature alone, regardless of concept or premise. If you are interested in writing a script for lower-budget companies and smaller independents — art films essentially — you will need to have an idea of what elements should be avoided.

Tip Sheet For Low-Budget Screenwriting —
www.communicator.com/scriptip.html
Colin Brunton of the Canadian Film Centre has put together the best presentation on low-budget writing found online.

SOFTWARE

When you're ready to pay a couple of hundred dollars for some professional script-formatting software, there are several to choose from. I think they are all very good and will do the job. If you're curious about which professional uses which program, visit each product's Web site for more information.

Movie Magic Screenwriter 2000 — *www.screenplay.com*
Final Draft — *www.finaldraft.com*

SCRIPT REVIEWS

Reviewing or analyzing produced screenplays is nothing new, but as far as the Web is concerned, it's a fairly new thing. My Web site is one of only a few that offer script reviews of films in development. I think it is beneficial for inexperienced screenwriters to learn what makes these produced screenplays so special. You can also learn how screenplays are sometimes stripped and diluted during development (by countless rewrites), to the point where the original vision of the screenwriter ceases to exist.

SU Script Reviews —
www.screenwritersutopia.com/script_reviews/sr_archive.html
Reviews present an overall impression of the material along with some basic critique. I think screenwriters can find reviews to be very helpful in learning more about the business and what makes a good screenplay. Some of the scripts reviewed include: *Pearl Harbor, Hannibal, Ocean's Eleven, The Salton Sea, The Panic Room*, and dozens more. (The link above takes you directly into the archive, so be sure to check the home page for the most recent reviews.)

Stax — *filmforce.ign.com/stax/*
Stax is probably the most respected and well-known script reviewer on the Web. His reviews can furnish writers with great insights into the development of the story, what's working and what's not, and who the major players are in the script's development — its director, producer, and actors.

Script Studies —
screenwriting.about.com/arts/screenwriting/cs/scriptstudies/index.htm
This is a great resource for writers interested in a more scholarly review of some of the better-produced screenplays. Analysis includes character development, story development, themes, and more.

THE READY-TO-SELL SCREENWRITER

We'd all like to think we're ready to jump into the snake pit and take our chances right now. Yes, you could sell your spec script, like Shane Black did with *Lethal Weapon*, and do so for a record price. You could also languish for years waiting for your first big break, as Frank Darabont did with *The Shawshank Redemption*. I'd like to think that as screenwriters, we'll know when we're ready, but often we lay back or charge ahead when we should do the opposite. At this point in your quest, you'll need information and advice on how to contact agents and producers, among other things. Oh yeah, and you're going to need some luck.

The Art of the Pitch —
www.cyberfilmschool.com/articles/perfect_pitch_x1.htm
Ken Rotcop runs the Professional Writers Workshop and created Pitchmart,™ an exciting session where production executives listen to pitches from aspiring screenwriters. This Web site includes an excerpt from his excellent book, *The Perfect Pitch*.

How Do You Get an Agent? —
wordplayer.com/pros/pr04a.Petrie.Dan.Jr.html
Another excellent column from the *WordPlay* Web site, this one is by
Dan Petrie Jr. who wrote *Beverly Hills Cop*. Several agents offer their
insights and advice.

Two Brads or Three? — *www.screentalk.org/art028.htm*
Elizabeth English, via the *ScreenTalk Magazine* Web site, offers
some food for thought before you start sending out your screenplay.

"You Don't Have To Live in Hollywood To Sell Your First Script!" —
www.screenwritersutopia.com/pros/callingcard.html
Andrea Leigh Wolf, author of *Sell Your Screenplay*, is a working screenwriter. She offers solid advice on how she made it as an unknown. And
get this: She sold the first script she ever wrote.

"Ten Tips for Successful Screenwriting" —
www.screenwritersutopia.com/pros/hollywoodscript.html
This is from script consultant Craig Kellem of *hollywoodscript.com*. Just
as the title says, these are ten tips you'll want to know.

"How To Be a Great Screenwriter" — *www.unmovies.com/howto.htm*
Professional screenwriter Daniel Knauf has a great site that offers advice
and humor to get you through the day. In his own words, "You'll notice
I said, 'anybody can learn to write a script.' This is analogous to saying,
'anybody can sing.' Unfortunately, simply because one has the ability to
execute a task, it doesn't necessarily follow that one will excel at said task."

"An Entertainment Script: Idea Through First Draft" —
www.screenstyle.com/screenstyle/fromcontofir.html
Here is an excellent online article by Jack Adams that originally appeared in
Creative Screenwriting magazine in 1994. It offers some great information
for you to mull over as you find your way as a screenwriter.

"Here's My Advice" — *home.earthlink.net/~scribbler/launer_advice.html*
Dale Launer's (*Ruthless People, Dirty Rotten Scoundrels, My Cousin Vinny*) first offering of advice is not to try. Then of course he goes on to give some poignant and noteworthy suggestions for all writers. This column is on Brad Mirman's site.

FINDING AN AGENT

For more on agents, including detailed listings, see Chapter Five.

The LiteraryAgent.Com — *nt9.nyic.com/literaryagent/sch-page.html*
This great database is fully searchable. Not only will you find agents interested in screenwriters, but ones looking for authors as well. To find agents and agencies interested in screenwriters, use their search device and simply type in "screenplays."

Literary Agents: Warnings and Cautions for Writers —
www.sfwa.org/beware/agents.html
Even though this page is geared more towards the publishing world, it still holds some value for you, the screenwriter. Many of the warnings offered here will apply to you as you search for an agent.

The View from the Other Side —
www.wga.org/WrittenBy/1996/0396/litagent.htm
Read what some of the leading literary agents in Hollywood have to say about the agent-writer relationship and what can be expected.

Writers Net: Literary Agents — *www.writers.net/agents.html*
One of the best resources for finding an agent, this site lists e-mail addresses and what each agent specializes in. There are many to chose from. The Writers Network does not list agents who admit to charging reader fees, so if any of them asks you to pay a reader fee, report it.

The Ink Spot Literary Agent Information —
www.inkspot.com/market/agents.html
An excellent resource with updated information on agent listings and other information. They have articles for you to review and links for finding legitimate agents. I highly recommend this site.

Literary Agent.com — *www.literaryagent.com/index.html*
Though it has a ways to go, keep your eye on this site. They need more participation from online agents, and I think they will get it.

CyberSpace Film School: Writer's Agent Listing —
hollywoodu.com/wagt.htm
A large list, but with no e-mail addresses and only general contact information that is really of little help unless you have a referral.

SUBMITTING YOUR SCRIPT

"Screenwriters Beware!" — *www.beverlyhillslit.com/insureadeal.html*
This is a reprint of an article by Michael Hauge. In it, he discusses the reality of approaching an agent.

WRITERS WANTED!

Here are some excellent options for finding agent and producer listings. These resources are good because it's the agent or producer who posts the listing, so you know they are looking for new writers right now. As always, be careful when dealing with unknown companies. For more on producers and production companies, including listings, see Chapter Six. For advice on how to contact agents and producers via e-mail, see Chapter Four.

TMe: Writers Wanted — *www.teako170.com/help1.html*
This site is updated the first week of every month. There are always a couple of dozen listings to review. All listings include an e-mail address, and most request you contact them with an e-mail query only.

Writers and Screenplays Wanted —
www.hollywoodlitsales.com/guestbooks/2/board2.html
Probably the best source online for current updated listings of producers and companies looking for new talent. This is an outstanding database that allows the individual person or company to post their own listing directly to the page.

The Hollydex — *actors.com/hn/directory/dirsearch/tview.html*
This database easily allows you to search for production companies, producers, or even agents. You can narrow your search by selecting "film" or "television."

The Ink Spot: Wanted Ads — *www.inkspot.com/classifieds/wanted.html*
Mixed in with ads for novelists and other writers, you will find an occasional agent or production company searching for new screenwriters.

Industry Companies Seeking Projects —
www.surfview.com/seindlst.htm
Another solid list, it contains mostly major production companies with some independents mixed in. The site offers past credits, budget range, and what kind of material each company is seeking.

P & E: Agent Listings — *www.blindside.net/P&E/*
This is an online guide to agents, as well as publishers and writing services. Although mainly a list of agents for novelists, I've found listings here for screenwriters as well.

HCDONLINE.COM JOB BOARD

I hope all of you have visited the *Hollywood Creative Directory* Web site. And if you're truly serious about making it as a writer, you'll fork out the $199.95 for the producers and production company listings, hundreds of which include e-mail addresses.[5]

But have you tried this? Go to their free Entertainment Job Board.[6] Once there, you'll notice a series of categories. First check out "Creative." Scan for something like "Executive Assistant," and click on it. Within each one of these job listings there is sometimes an e-mail address (listed at the bottom) for the producer, executive, agent, or current assistant of that company. Click on the e-mail link and send them a blind e-mail query. (See Chapter Four.)

The "Creative" board won't have many listings and isn't the best option, but it is always worth a shot. Now check out "Interns." Here's where the real possibilities exist. I've noticed that production companies and agencies tend to list their e-mail addresses here more often. Why? They're looking for young people willing to work for nothing or very little, and they realize posting their e-mail address is a good way to get more responses. Most young people will be inclined to send an e-mail as opposed to faxing a resume.

Scan down the list of intern jobs. There could be upwards of 80 to 100 listings here. Start selecting ones that seem to come from a production company or agency. Look specifically for "Development Intern" listings. The day of this writing there were a half dozen of them, and four had e-mail addresses. The development department is in charge of the acquiring and reading of scripts. The e-mail address listed here will go directly to the current intern or assistant, or maybe even the Vice President of Development.

You won't find addresses in these listings, but you will find fax and phone numbers. Fax tends to be the preferred way to send a resume, but e-mail is a close second. As for phone calls, "absolutely no phone calls" is stated in almost half of the listings.

---

[5] *www.hcdonline.com*
[6] *www.hcdonline.com/jobs/default.asp*

If you're looking for an e-mail address for an agent, there is an "Agents & Managers" board that always produces some leads.

The great thing about all of these listings is that they are located in California. You'll very rarely see a listing for some company in Miami or Chicago. The bottom line is that your chances of success here are not always good, but you need a break, and it can happen anywhere.

Don't just stop here; check out magazine sites, which often have "Classifieds" or job listings areas as well.

THE SCRIPT READER

There is no one more feared by screenwriters than the reader/story analyst. Getting your script past them is the key. Here are some things you should keep in mind when you are writing your script.

Inside Film: Screenwriting — *www.insidefilm.com/screenwriting.html*
This site offers more than just articles on Hollywood script readers and query letters; it also covers the screenwriting craft. Susan Royal keeps the site updated regularly with excellent offerings. The article I want to point out is from the Hollywood Film Conference and deals with the story analysit. *www.insidefilm.com/hollywoodfilmfest.html*

See Your Script Through the Reader's Eyes —
hollywoodnet.com/Hauge/readers.html
When getting ready to approach a reader, producer, or agent, there are several things you should keep in mind. Author Michael Hauge presents some guidelines and advice that could help you increase the chances of getting your screenplay read favorably.

Death to Readers —
www.wordplayer.com/columns/wp05.Death.to.Readers.html
Professional screenwriter Terry Rossio confesses that he himself was a dreaded reader for two years. But most importantly Mr. Rossio provides an incredibly in-depth "checklist" for you to mull over.

MORE INTERVIEWS

Here are some select interviews that should interest you, which offer unique points of view. Again, anytime you have the opportunity to read what a professional has to say, you should take advantage of it. Below you will find some of the best interviews the Web has to offer.

True Beauty: Interview with Alan Ball —
www.wga.org/writtenBy/0300/ball.html
Nicholas Kazan talks with Oscar-winner Alan Ball about his original screenplay, *American Beauty*. It's a great interview that plots the script's journey from sale to production, brought to you by *Written By* magazine.

William Goldman Interview —
www.screenwritersutopia.com/interviews/goldman_interview.html
Moriarty from *aintitcoolnews.com* conducted a great interview with one of the working legends of the screenwriting profession. Mr. Goldman offers his opinions and observations of some of the important movies of 2000. He also discusses the state of the industry.

Interview with Rich Whiteside —
www.screenwritersutopia.com/interviews/scrnlife.html
I had a chance to interview Rich Whiteside, the author of *The Screenwriting Life: The Dream, the Job and the Reality*, whom I found to be very fascinating. If you are ever fortunate enough to work in Hollywood, this is one of the interviews you should read — honest and straightforward.

Method Writing: An Interview with Quentin Tarantino —
www.creativescreenwriting.com/interviews/tarantino4,30,99.html
No other screenwriter in recent memory has captured the imagination of his fans like Quentin Tarantino. From *Creative Screenwriting Magazine* comes a must-read by Erik Bauer for every aspiring screenwriter.

Ben Younger: The Power of Words —
www.nyscreenwriter.com/article49.htm
Ben Younger's story is an inspiration to us all. While working as a waiter at a New York City restaurant, he wrote and fine-tuned his only script, *Boiler Room*. One of the restaurant regulars was a professional screenwriter who offered his help. Not long after, Ben was done working as a waiter.

Walking The Mile II: An Interview with Frank Darabont —
www.creativescreenwriting.com/interviews/darabont_1299.html
One of the best interviews online is Daniel Argent's Q & A with Frank Darabont (*The Shawshank Redemption*), whose journey to the top of the screenwriting spectrum was anything but a sure thing. He was one of those ten-years-in-the-making "overnight" success stories.

Interview Excerpt — Frank Darabont on how he starts his day of writing: "I start every day by pulling out yesterday's pages and revisiting them; copyediting and then inputting changes and reworking things. I'll do that for an hour or two in the morning, because that gets me back up to speed. I understand that's not uncommon amongst writers. The danger is that you wind up reworking everything you've done so far and you spend an entire day doing that."

Bo Zenga: The Pitch King Produces —
www.creativescreenwriting.com/interviews/bozenga09,01,99.html
Bo Zenga, "The Pitch King," as he has been called, could teach all of us a thing or two about pitching. When you get to the point where you're ready to start pitching your script, consult this excellent interview. Anyone who can sell their first pitch, as Bo Zenga did, has to know what they're doing.

Christopher McQuarrie —
www.teleport.com/~cdeemer/interview-cmq.html
This interview is by DiAnne Olson. Christopher McQuarrie is one of
the best screenwriters, now a director, working today. His script for *The
Usual Suspects* will forever be regarded as a classic. I encourage every
struggling writer to read the script, see the movie, and read this interview.

A Walk On The Wild Side: An Interview with Brad Mirman —
www.screenwritersutopia.com/interviews/kenna1.html
Interviewer Kenna McHugh does a great job of pulling out some useful
information and advice from Brad Mirman for beginning and advanced
screenwriters to consider.

Interview Excerpt — Brad Mirman on how he knows if a scene is working
or not: "Sometimes it is very hard to know. There are times when I just
get a very vague feeling that something is wrong with a scene, but I can't
put my finger on it. I usually step away from the screenplay for a few days
and it comes to me. I know other writers who just move on to the next
scene and come back to the scene that is giving them problems. This is
something I can't do. Since a screenplay is one, interrelated work... what
you write in one scene can put the spin on scenes that follow."

An Interview with Christopher Lambert —
home.earthlink.net/~scribbler/lambert.html
This interview appears on Brad Mirman's site. Christopher Lambert
(*Greystoke, Highlander, Knight Moves, Mortal Kombat, Nirvana*) worked
with Mirman on several films and shares some of those experiences.
Lambert offers good insights into storytelling and other aspects of
screenwriting, including collaborations.

The Art of Storytelling —
www.screenwritersutopia.com/interviews/delso002.html
Michael B. Druxman, screenwriter of *The Doorway* (director as well),
Cheyenne Warrior, and *Dillinger and Capone* has been a very active online
personality, offering his time willingly. Gregg Delso conducts this interview
with Druxman, who shares his thoughts on storytelling.

<u>Interview Excerpt</u> — Mr. Druxman explains his writing schedule: "I usually do my best writing in the morning, after I walk my dog, drink my coffee, and read the paper. I'll write for two to three hours, then stop the actual writing for the day. However, for the rest of the afternoon and evening, I'm planning what I will do the next morning. When I sit down at the computer, I always know what I'm going to write, so that I get my work done quickly."

GENERAL RESOURCES

MAGAZINES

Magazine Web sites usually offer interviews and samples from their current issues. Most will have additional information that you cannot find in the magazine. None of them offers a Web subscription that allows you to read the entire magazine online for a fee, which is too bad, as I think that's really the direction that they should be heading as far as Web site development goes.

Written By — *www.wga.org/writtenBy*
This is the Writers Guild of America magazine for Guild members, but anyone can subscribe to it. The WGA site has a great collection of interviews available from current and back issues.

Fade In Magazine — *www.fadeinmag.com*
They offer articles and an occasional interview from their current issues and back issues on the site.

Script Magazine — *www.scriptmag.com*
They have a nice free e-zine with articles, columns, and interviews not found in the magazine. Site also includes book, movie, and script reviews.

Creative Screenwriting — *www.creativescreenwriting.com*
A great collection of interviews to browse, this also offers script reviews and articles covering virtually every aspect of screenwriting.

New York Screenwriter — *www.nyscreenwriter.com*
One of the better magazine Web sites, it features regular updates and a good selection of interviews from current and back issues.

ScreenTalk — *www.screentalk.org*
Geared towards the "international" screenwriter, *ScreenTalk* has developed into a nice niche publication. They are kind of the new kids on the block, as they just recently went from electronic to print. They have interviews and articles, and their site is always well maintained. They also have a large collection of produced movie scripts to download for free.

Hollywood Script Writer — *www.hollywoodscriptwriter.com*
"The only trade paper specifically for screenwriters" has a nice Web site with interviews, columns, and discussion groups.

SCREENWRITING COMPETITIONS

Winning a major screenwriting competition is one of the fastest ways to start a screenwriting career. Some contests offer fellowships or internships where you are paid a stipend for up to a year that allows you to write more than you ever have, and in addition, you are often assigned a mentor and establish industry contacts. Winning any legitimate contest can help you separate yourself from the pack of other screenwriters. When you start writing query letters and you can list yourself as a finalist or winner of a competition, your letter will be given more attention. (See our interview with Thom Taylor, author of *The Big Deal: Hollywood's Million-Dollar Spec Script Market*, in Chapter Ten.)

Select wisely when you set out to enter a competition. Weigh the submission fee against what you can gain from the competition and how many winners there are. Also, be sure to read the guidelines and rules for every contest. There could be restrictions that apply to you. Finally, be sure to submit your screenplay in proper format and bound together with brass brads. Here is a list of a few of the major competitions out there. For the most comprehensive list of competitions available, visit *moviebytes.com*.

Academy of Television Arts & Sciences Student Internship Program
5220 Lankershim Blvd.
North Hollywood, CA 91601-3109
(818) 754-2830
Web Address: *www.emmys.org/eps*
E-mail: *internships@emmys.org*

Comments: Last year's deadline was in March of 2000. Check their Web site for the current deadline. A $2,500 stipend for each internship is awarded. Interns from outside of L.A. County are eligible for an additional $500 for travel and housing.

American Accolades Screenwriting Competition
2118 Wilshire Blvd., Suite 160
Santa Monica, CA 90403
(310) 453-2523
Web Address: *www.americanaccolades.com*
E-mail: *info@americanaccolades.com*

Comments: Deadline is in the spring each year. Check their Web site for the exact date. They give out over $5,000 in cash and prizes, with a Grand Prize of $2,500. They also offer other gifts and awards as well.

American Screenwriters Association
269 S. Beverly Drive, Suite 2600
Beverly Hills, CA 90212-3807
(866) 265-9091
Web Address: *www.asascreenwriters.com*
E-mail: *asa@asascreenwriters.com*

Comments: Deadline is December 31st of every year. They give away cash, prizes, and gifts. Most important, the Grand Prize winner gets a free trip to the annual *Selling to Hollywood Screenwriters Conference.* Travel, including airfare, is covered.

Austin Film Festival Screenplay Competition
(800) 310-FEST
(512) 478-4795
Web Address: *www.austinfilmfestival.org*

Comments: Visit their Web site for current fees and guidelines. One First Place winner gets a $4,000 cash prize and participation in the AFF Mentor Program as well as reimbursement of one round-trip airfare (up to $500) to the festival. They also give each winner a complimentary all-access pass to the festival and conference.

The Chesterfield Film Company
Writers Film Project
1158 26th Street, Box 544
Santa Monica, CA 90403
(213) 683-3977
Web Address: *www.chesterfield-co.com*
E-mail: *info@chesterfield-co.com*

Comments: The deadline for 2001 applications was May 15th. Visit their Web site for the latest details. The Writers Film Project (WFP) was started in 1990 in conjunction with Amblin Entertainment (Steven Spielberg's company) and Universal Pictures. This fellowship offers fiction, theater, and film writers the opportunity to begin a career.

Those chosen to participate in the WFP receive a $20,000 fellowship stipend and participation in a year-long fellowship under the guidance of professional screenwriters and executive mentors.

Columbus Screenplay Discovery Awards
433 North Camden Drive, Suite 600
Beverly Hills, CA 90210
(310) 288-1988
Web Address: *www.hollywoodnetwork.com*
E-mail: *awards@hollywoodnetwork.com*

Comments: Submissions are accepted monthly. The final deadline for all submissions is in December of every year. A winner is selected each month and becomes a finalist for the year-end awards, when cash prizes are presented.

Nicholl Fellowships in Screenwriting
Academy Foundation
8949 Wilshire Blvd.
Beverly Hills, CA 90211-1972
(310) 247-3059
Web Address: *www.oscars.org/nicholl/index.html*

Comments: The deadline is May 1st of every year. The Nicholl Fellowships is an international competition open to screenwriters who have not earned more than $5,000 writing for film or television. Up to five $25,000 fellowships are awarded each year.

Walt Disney Studios/ABC Writers Fellowship
500 South Buena Vista Street
Burbank, CA 91521-0705
(818) 560-6894
Web Address: *www.abcnewtalent.disney.com*

Comments: There is a submission period effective from June 1 to June 21, 2001. Check the Web site for current guidelines. They offer fellowships in the feature film and television areas. A $33,000 salary will be provided for a one-year period.

Writers Network Screenplay Competition
289 South Robertson Blvd.
Beverly Hills, CA 90211
(800) 646-3896
E-mail: *writersnet@aol.com*

Comments: The previous deadline was in May of 2000. Use the e-mail address above to contact them for current guidelines. They usually give out cash awards of up to $2,500.

Writer's Digest Annual Writing Competition
Dept MB
1507 Dana Avenue
Cincinnati, OH 45207
(513) 531-2690
Web Address: *www.writersdigest.com/catalog/2000wdcontest_text.html*
E-mail: *competitions@fwpubs.com*

Comments: The deadline is usually in the spring of every year. Overall contest prizes total more than $25,000. Visit the Web site for full details.

PROJECT GREENLIGHT

About two years ago, a guy named Alex Keledjian came up with an original idea to have a TV show chronicle the making of a film by a first-time filmmaker. He was himself a frustrated filmmaker living in Hollywood when one day, while watching MTV's *The Real World*, the idea came to him.

"He could make a movie for the money they spend on that house," is what he thought. "And it would probably be more interesting to watch than a bunch of kids whining," says Eli Holzman of Miramax.

Here's how it works. You can submit your screenplay for no fee. However, you can't be a produced screenwriter or filmmaker. From entries submitted by thousands of aspiring screenwriters and filmmakers, they will, through a long examining process that includes prospective finalists having to make a video of a scene from their script, select one winner who will direct his or her original screenplay for Miramax films. The entire production of the film will be covered in an HBO documentary-style television series.

"We had just started Miramax's TV division, so when I heard Alex's idea, I knew it could be the perfect project for us," says Holzman. "I brought it to my boss, Miramax TV president Billy Campbell."

Soon thereafter they shared the idea with Kent Kubena, who just happened to work for Matt Damon, Ben Affleck, and Chris Moore. "When he [Billy Campbell] brought it to them and they wanted to be involved, we knew we had a winner," adds Holzman.

They spent six months working out the details for how the contest would work. "Finally we arrived at something of a consensus, and we brought the idea to HBO."

The contest officially launched in September of 2000. Quickly, thousands of writers began filling out the entry form and submitting their screenplays. In February of 2001, the project had announced ten finalists whose short scenes shot on video will be reviewed by Matt Damon and Ben Affleck. From those ten, a final three will be selected, and then the winner will get to direct his or her movie.[7]

ESSENTIAL ELEMENTS

Everything you need to start a screenwriting career, including script supplies, software, books, tapes, and videos, can be ordered on the Web. You can even register for a professional class or seminar at some online stores. When you need a book or some software, consider ordering from stores designed to fit the needs of writers specifically (such as the ones listed below), instead of a megastore. You'll find the prices, service, and quality to be the same, if not better.

---

[7] *www.projectgreenlight.com*

The Writer's Store — *www.writersstore.com*
Formerly known as The Writer's Computer Store, this is a family-run store that is professional and reliable. The Writer's Store is the number one location in the Los Angeles area to buy all of your screenwriting supplies. If you happen to be out West, stop by and see friendly owners Gabriele, Dan, and Jesse.

The Writers Store
2040 Westwood Blvd.
Los Angeles, CA 90025
(800) 272-8927
E-mail: *sales@writersstore.com*

ScreenStyle — *www.screenstyle.com*
Screen Style started out as a software company before expanding into an online store. They are an excellent source for software and other supplies and pride themselves on quality customer sevice.

SCREENWRITING AND HOLLYWOOD NEWS

While it is very important that you keep on top of what's happening in Hollywood and what kind of material is hot, I don't agree with those who say you should pay attention to trends. There are even some who suggest you should write to the market. Only in extremely rare cases would this do you any good. The reality is that by the time something is hot, you've already missed out. The only exception would be if you were lucky enough to have written such material already.

There are some sites that can give you a very advanced notice of possible trends in what will be hot on the spec market, like my site, but I do not recommend that you try to anticipate and write something for that reason alone. Unless you are being paid to do otherwise, always write what you know and what you are passionate about.

Keeping up with the daily news from Hollywood is important so you'll know who runs which studio, who's buying what, and who the top agents are. If you are ever in a situation where you need to know this stuff, you'll be ready.

For most of us, it's all part of being a screenwriter. I love to know what films are in development, who sold what, and for how much, and I enjoy reading screenplays that are in development. It's more fun than serious.

Dark Horizons — *www.darkhorizons.com*
Editor Garth Franklin runs a very tight ship. I consider his site to be the most professional of the bunch. Very rarely does he take part in rumor-running. His site is updated daily and includes industry news, movie and DVD reviews, and script reviews.

Coming Attractions — *www.corona.bc.ca/films/mainFramed.html*
Probably one of the most unassuming news sites, and one of the best, the site is based in Vancouver and is run by its owner, Patrick Sauriol. From the site: "Don't be fooled by the fact we're not based in Hollywood. Coming Attractions has field correspondents in Los Angeles, New York City, Atlanta, Montreal, and Tokyo, as well as Vancouver, so we easily achieve a global film audience." They are also the original database source for movies in development.

AICN — *www.aintitcoolnews.com*
The biggest movie news/gossip personality on the Web is Harry Knowles, and with good reason. He has done a spectacular job marketing himself and his site, Aint It Cool News, (AICN), from the funny little animated cartoon of himself (you can't miss it), to his uncanny knack for getting invited to movie sets and premieres. Studios seem to find it beneficial to invite him, in the hope that he will write something positive about the film on his site.

Knowles and his site have been much maligned of late. *Film Threat* magazine did an exposé piece on him last year, entitled, "Deconstructing

Harry." In it, Harry was exposed for certain things he and his fellow "geeks" have done, some quite embarrassing. Yet Harry's popularity is as great as ever. What separates his site from the others is his network of "spies" who bring him tasty news bits about films in development. He is constantly getting his hands on information that no one else has.

In 1999, Knowles reached his ascendance in power and fame when *Premiere* magazine acknowledged him in its "100 Most Powerful People in Hollywood" issue. Coming in at number 98, Knowles was the first Web site operator and owner to make such a list on those merits alone.

There are legendary tales of Aint It Cool News dooming movies before they were ever released. With roughly two million monthly readers, they can create an incredible backlash. By posting negative reviews from test screenings, he and his followers have been accused of turning the tide against some movies. Negative reviews generate negative buzz. It's a domino effect that some movies never recover from. On top of that, it all happens months before the movie is released, thereby ensuring that there is time for the negative reviews to spread.

So what happens when a movie receives positive Web reviews? *The Blair Witch Project* received a rave review from Knowles. A movie almost no one was talking about until Knowles posted his review became one of the biggest surprises in movie history. Whether or not AICN has that much of an impact is debatable, but what isn't is the fact that Hollywood is paying close attention to what he says.

Screenwriters Utopia — *www.screenwritersutopia.com*
This site focuses on the screenwriter — from script sales to reviews, news, and script reports. Also includes interviews with some of the top screenwriters in the business.

Done Deal — *www.scriptsales.com*
The number one source on the Web for script sales, they also have some nice interviews and an archive of past sales going back to 1997.

Movie Headlines — *www.movieheadlines.net*
Another great source for movie news and gossip, this site includes script, movie, and DVD reviews.

Upcomingmovies — *www.upcomingmovies.com*
You just know that another *Rambo* movie is in development, it might even be filming right now, but you're not sure. Maybe you're a big fan of that Rambo character. Well, for information on movies in development, check out this great resource. If they don't have it listed, then it probably isn't in the works.

Film Threat — *www.filmthreat.com*
Chris Gore is one of the more prominent media figures in independent film. He is the publisher of *Film Threat* magazine, editor of the *All-Movie Guide*, has his own TV show, and writes numerous columns. The *Film Threat* Web site keeps you on top of the independent film industry like nothing else can. The site features reviews and interviews and keeps you up to date on what's playing in theaters across the country. Sign up for their e-newsletter to receive "indie" news in your mailbox every week.

Indiewire — *www.indiewire.com*
Started in 1995 as a small Internet e-publication (let's face it, they were all small back in 1995), it has since developed into a leading voice of independent film. They too have a great e-newsletter featuring reviews and interviews, for which you should sign up as well.

4filmmakers — *www.4filmmakers.com*
This could be the site to watch — a comprehensive database for movies in development. There are dozens of new entries and updates every day. 4filmmakers is quickly becoming the source for information on projects in development.

Variety — *www.variety.com*

If you really want to stay on top of what's happening in Hollywood, you'll fork out the thirty-three-dollar-per-month fee for their Variety Extra online edition. If you can't afford that, then sign up for their "Free Daily e-mail Service," which e-mails you all of the headlines on the front page, along with a few stories you can read.

Who's Buying What — *www.moviebytes.com/sales/subscribe.cfm*

This is one of the premiere services on the Web for information on what agents are selling what material and who is buying it: producers, production companies, and studios. It's a massive database with thousands of listings. You will be required to pay for access, but you can get free access for a day to try it out before you have to pay.

CHAPTER FOUR

THE E-MAIL QUERY

You've written a half dozen screenplays and you've honed and crafted them to the point where you're now ready to start submitting. Finding the right agent, producer, or production company to submit your project to will be the hardest part. You will find that the blood, sweat, and tears of the past two or three years have been nothing. You are now going to face rejection, and lots of it. You will not have your phone calls returned — that is, if you're lucky enough to leave a message with anyone of importance. You will also find that the gatekeepers will happily slap up wall after wall to slow you down. Soon after, you'll start to doubt yourself.

With that said, you can do it! After reading this chapter, you will increase the odds of your e-mail query having success. You can get your screenplay in front of a set of eyeballs that are attached to a head that is resting on the shoulders of someone who could either buy your screenplay or sign you as a client.

E-mail is the most popular written form of communication in the world. Over thirty million reach their destination every day. E-mail is used on a daily basis to conduct business in Hollywood — and everywhere else for that matter.

When you send off a letter on paper, you're reviewing screenwriting textbooks for how-to information on query letters. Yet some of you are using e-mail to contact agents and producers without giving it a second thought. Your e-mail query must be given the same amount of thought and respect. When you query an agent or producer through e-mail, there are some things you should know. There are strategies you can use to increase your odds of success.

THE LETTER VERSUS E-MAIL

My strategy is different with e-mail querying, compared to the letter form. E-mail is a relatively new way of contacting agents and producers. The rules are not yet clearly defined. There are dozens of books that offer tips, suggestions, and outright rules for writers interested in querying with a letter.

Writer/producer Richard Finney has noticed a consistent "system" developing among the more experienced writers who contact his company. "They e-mail me and request the opportunity to query me. They usually include some information about themselves. Sometimes they mention the genre of the material. I reply by e-mail that I am open to queries. They write again with their ideas, or a brief description of their script or treatment. I look at it and usually respond within a day."

Producers like Richard Finney have been utilizing e-mail for years, and even prefer it over letters and faxes. The main reason: E-mail will wait for them. They can check it at their leisure. "I can respond to an e-mail query upon my convenience," says Finney.

"I prefer e-mail queries. E-mail is easier to read, respond, and delete," confirms Director of Development for Simon Tse Productions, Jill Nowak.

What with meetings, phone calls, faxes, and certified mail arriving constantly, it's not hard to imagine why. Finney agrees, "The ranking of contact methods for me personally goes like this: e-mail, phone, fax, letter. Certified mail seems over the top." More and more producers and agents are turning to e-mail as not just a means of doing business, but as a primary way of establishing relationships with writers and other professionals.

"It's weird how by using e-mail you can strike up a relationship with an executive or a producer that you might never achieve over the phone," remarks Finney. "Last night I was sitting with a director that we are shooting a movie with, who told my producing partner and I that the first contact he had with us was through our Web site."

Frederick Levy, vice president of development at Marty Katz Productions, sees e-mail as only continuing to be a more significant force in the moviemaking process, "Instead of calling back and forth a million times per day, I can e-mail back and forth. We're doing a movie right now called *Frailty* that Bill Paxton is directing. I can e-mail the director, other producers on the project, and my line producer."

E-mail is a completely different beast than a letter. A letter is more formal, more elegant. I concede it is still the best way to contact agents. But with that said, the first agent I signed with was a contact I made from an e-mail query. Still, just because you are sending an e-mail does not mean it is a less important document. Take your e-mail correspondences seriously because the producer or agent on the other end will.

Perhaps the most significant thing about e-mail is that it usually finds its way to the producer, not some assistant. Anything that comes from the mailroom or fax machine is almost always first dealt with by an assistant. "I have a story editor who deals with all of the fax and query letters, but I read all of my own e-mail," says Levy. Your goal is to circumvent as many middlemen as possible, and e-mail can help you do that.

More than anything else, the phone is the biggest loser in today's Internet world. Especially with the proliferation of voicemail, you can almost never get an agent or producer on the line. They will always be screening their calls.

This chapter is primarily focused on contacting the independent producer and/or the smaller production company. You will not have any success e-mailing Miramax chairman Harvey Weinstein — that's if you even had his e-mail address. Focus on the smaller production companies and independent producers, like the ones listed in Chapter Six.

In the traditional query letter, you're allotted three or four paragraphs. It's recommended that you open up your letter with your premise statement, log line, or central question. Your movie idea is best presented if it is of the high-concept variety. You'll also want to introduce the main character(s), then some kind of a hook. The genre and title of the work must be apparent as well. It is also recommend that you provide a little information about yourself and what, if any, credentials you have. Then the letter is wrapped up with a plea to whoever-it-is to read your script, along with your contact information.

In a typical query letter, your goal is to separate yourself from the pack in a few paragraphs. With e-mail, you don't have that much time! The majority of producers and agents you'll run into on the Internet will not read e-mail of excessive length. No one likes to get a full page of e-mail from someone they do not know.

COMMON SENSE STILL APPLIES

There are some commonalties between e-mail and the letter. Always be on the lookout for scams. *You should never have to pay for an agent or production company to review your screenplay.* Never, ever, ever. Here are some other common-sense things you should know:

- Never send your script without permission. If you send an unsolicited script, it won't get read; it won't even be opened. Do not attach an entire script to an e-mail. I once had a very reputable producer ask me to submit the first ten pages of my script to him via e-mail. I did, but do not recommend it. I can't imagine someone asking you to do that.

- Don't be arrogant in your communication; avoid proclamations: "I can write better than what I've seen at the movies"; "I'm the best screen-writer nobody's ever heard of"; "My script will win the Academy Award for Best Original Screenplay."

- Pay attention to details and follow instructions. When you see a post on a "Writers Wanted" board or find a company's Web site, be sure to look closely for submission guidelines. "I posted on *holly-woodlitsales.com* that we were looking for scripts," says producer Michael Grace. "I asked that everyone place 'RE: Hollywoodlitsales' in the subject header, and only about 20% bothered to do it. Writers need to pay attention to details. If they can't pay attention to details when querying, how well do they do it in their script?"

- Do not instruct them to visit your Web site to read your log lines or synopsis; they will not go. Do include a link at the bottom of your e-mail in your signature file (see below) but do not get lazy and ask them to go to your Web site and read something. If they are curious about you, they might visit your home page. Leave it up to them.

- Be professional, patient, and courteous.

If you're pitching a comedy script, try to do so with some humor, but avoid using jokes — especially bad ones. I would also eschew witty monologues or catchy phrases unless it is somehow worked into your comedy pitch. I used to have a saying attached to my e-mail signature file that read, "If you're not a part of the solution, then you're part of the problem." I had e-mailed a producer who promptly responded by cutting me down to size. He informed me that he could tell I was an amateur by my "unprofessional" e-mail, and I obviously had no idea how to approach someone of his stature. Well, needless to say, he did not request my script. He was harsh, but he was also correct. Don't risk offending anyone. Also, be patient. It takes a little time for agents or producers to get back to you. Be courteous, even when rejected. Always be the bigger person. You'll feel better in the end.

E-MAIL SIGNATURE FILE

An e-mail signature file appears at the end of your e-mail and is automatically placed there by your browser. While in Netscape, go to: *edit > preferences > identity*, and there you will see a signature-file window. Then enter the location of your signature text file.[1] Here is an example:

Your Name
Your E-mail
Your Home Page Address
Telephone Number

---

[1] In Outlook Express, go to: *tools > options > signatures*.

Your signature file usually consists of your contact information and home page address, the stuff that you want attached to almost every e-mail and want to avoid having to type every time. If you do not want your signature file to go out with a particular piece of e-mail, simply erase it from the message window after you click on New Message.

YOUR CONTACT PORTFOLIO

The goal of your e-mail query is to procure a response, even if it's a "No thanks." You need to build a portfolio of contacts. I guarantee you that your list of e-mail addresses will be greater than postal addresses. Being organized will make a big difference. You do not want to e-mail the same person the same message twice. Keeping track of who you have contacted, how long ago, and what the outcome of the contact was will be very important.

Here is an example:

Contact Name	Date	E-mail Address	Web Site	Outcome
Mr. Big	4/11/00	mrbig@independent.com	indyfilm.com	Query sent
	4/14/00			Requested synopsis
	4/15/00			Sent synopsis
	4/18/00			Requested script!

By keeping a portfolio of each contact's name, e-mail, Web site, mailing address, dates of contact, outcome, and follow-up information, you can chart your contact movement.

WRITING THE E-MAIL QUERY

Keep your e-mail query short and to the point. Think of your short e-mail correspondence as an exercise in word attrition. That's a big difference between the letter and e-mail. Do not describe your story in any way, shape, or form until asked to do so. Sometimes you can start right off with your log line or synopsis. Producer Adam Kline requests that you send "a five- to seven-sentence summary of each feature-length script," but for the most part, you'll want permission. Here are some basics for a successful e-mail query letter:

- What you place in your e-mail subject header is important. I have used "query," or simply "RE:" with nothing else. Less is usually more in this regard.

- Address whom it is you're contacting personally. If you don't have a contact name, address your e-mail to "Development" or "To Whom it may Concern." (Note: It is a very big plus if you can address someone specifically.)

- Do not announce you are a screenwriter. That will be obvious.

- Are you "repped"? This is important. If you're lucky enough to have a representative or agent, mention that right away. It puts production companies and producers more at ease. They like to avoid lawsuits, and when material is submitted through a WGA-sanctioned agent, there are protections involved. Also, if you're good enough to sign with an agent, right away you've separated yourself from the pack.

- Make a connection. (see below)

- Tell them the genre of your story, but do not describe it until asked to do so.

- Ask the question, "Are you accepting screenplay submissions?" (If you know they are, then omit this part and get right into your pitch.)

- Thank them for their time.

- Shut up and do a spellcheck. (Avoid misspelling someone's name; people likely will not respond if you can't even spell their name correctly.)

MAKE THE CONNECTION

I truly feel this is far more important with e-mail than a letter. E-mail is easily deleted; that's another reason why it is liked. You have to grab their attention right away, and be quick so as not to lose them. If you mention a film produced by the company or a successful client whom you admire, this will increase the chances of eliciting a response. When you do your homework and can mention credits or perhaps name-drop, you make a connection that most beginning writers do not bother to make. When an agent or producer sees someone who has gone the extra mile, they respect that and often will respond.

Research can easily be done by visiting a company's Web site, visiting message boards and checking out the rumor mill on ***news:misc.writing.screenwriting***. Here are some excellent resources for you:

Internet Movie database — easily look up credits (*imdb.com*)

SU Message Boards — screenwriters wanted board, production company listings (*screenwritersutopia.com*)

Corona Productions — films in development (*corona.ca.com*)

4Filmmakers — great resource to find out what a production company has under development. You do have to register, but it's free. (*4filmmakers.com*)

(For more resources, see Chapter Three.)

Normally you're not going to have much success when you send your drama piece about abortion to someone known for action films, so do your research.

Name-dropping and research are not the only ways to make a connection. Often you will provide everything that is necessary for a connection to be made. You'll write a marvelous synopsis or log line. You're a produced writer with credits, or you're a fresh young writer with some credentials.

CREDENTIALS

You don't have to be a produced or optioned screenwriter to have *credentials*. Have you placed in a screenwriting competition? Any writing competition, for that matter? Do you have any filmmaking experience? Even if it was in high school — or maybe as a kid you used to take your parents' old 8mm camera, write up a script, and shoot five-minute short films. You can find a way to work that in. Perhaps you were published, even if it was a small local paper. Maybe your play was produced by a local college or high school. These are all credentials and can be mentioned.

EDUCATION

I do not mention the fact that I have a degree in history and attended graduate school. I really feel it is a waste of precious time and space and does not increase my standing as a screenwriter. However, if you graduated from NYU film school or the UCLA screenwriting program, of course mention that. To me, that type of experience falls more under credentials. You've really accomplished something and most likely completed a short film or entered a prestigious school writing competition.

THE QUERY

I've given you as much detail as necessary for constructing your e-mail query. It's time to provide some examples. Remember, what I've outlined above are not rules, but starting points. You'll develop your own style, and you'll find that incorporating what you've learned here will be a major element.

Here's an example of a short query I've used with much success:

Dear John Jones,

*I am represented by Signed, Sealed & Delivered Literary Agency
in Bel Air. I am interested in submitting an action/adventure
screenplay to your company. I really enjoyed your film* _____
*and I feel I have something you might be interested in. Are
you currently accepting submissions? I'd be happy to send a log
line or synopsis. Thank you for your time.*

Sincerely,
Screenwriter

I used the above query when I had no idea if a company was accepting submissions. Here's another possible query offering a little more information.

Dear John Jones,

*As a winner in the Screenwriting Showcase Awards
and a fledgling filmmaker with several short films
completed, I would like to submit my action script
to your company. I really enjoyed your film* _____
*and feel I have something you might be interested in.
May I send more information to you about my screenplay,
including a log line and one-page synopsis?*

Sincerely,
Screenwriter

This producer makes action films. With the first e-mail, I've made the connection by mentioning one of his films. I also let him know I am represented, and I ask the question. In the second query, I do not have an agent so I start off strong with a couple of my biggest accomplishments. I was purposely vague about my filmmaking, but honest. I make the connection, I do not ramble on, and the question is proposed — very simple and straightforward.

90

He may not be interested in reading my script right away, or he may not be accepting submissions at this time, but if he responds the door is still open.

As it turned out, one of my respondents was in the middle of "development hell" on a new project. He asked me to contact him in three months. I did and managed to stay in touch with him. For some time, he was someone that I could submit to when appropriate. If I had been pushy and kept e-mailing every week, he would have stopped corresponding. Don't always assume producers are blowing you off just because they do not want to read your script immediately.

Here is an example of a query letter to an agent:

Dear Sally Agent,

As a winner in the Screenwriting Showcase Awards and a fledgling filmmaker with several short films completed, I would like to submit my action script to your company. I really admire your client _____, and feel I have something you might be interested in. May I send more information to you about my screenplay, including a log line and one-page synopsis? I have eight screenplays completed that can be reviewed.

Sincerely,
Screenwriter

With agents, you may find that they will ask you to send them a formal query letter. But generally, if they list their e-mail address on a Web site or you find it in an online directory, you should give e-mail a shot first before a letter.

Remember to use your "signature file," and if you can't do that, be sure to type your contact information including full name, address, e-mail address, and phone number, at the bottom of your e-mail. According to author/screenwriter Jenna Glatzer, "it's foolish to not provide all of your contact information, because if the recipient is interested, he or she will probably want to contact you immediately."

THE "LAUNDRY LIST"

Some writers — and even producers — refer to e-mail queries as "pitches." E-mail is easy to use, efficient, and requires less time to open, read, and discard than formal letters. So the pitch mentality is understandable — and it's why my suggestions to you are to be quick and to the point. Sending a batch of log lines to producers is sometimes all that is required. Screenwriter Genie Davis, who has had success with her e-mail pitches, explains. "I'd send to any producer who posted on the Internet for a type of project that I had available. Frankly, when I had time, anyone in the HCD (*Hollywood Creative Directory*) with an e-mail address would be sent a sentence about me and a laundry list of my log lines. I know, people say you're not supposed to do that, and obviously I would not send supernatural thrillers to a company that did only 'teen,' but if I had no idea as to genre, I'd laundry-list them all."

Typically the "laundry list" method is only useful when you have already contacted the producer with a short, formal e-mail query letter (shown above). Producer Jill Nowak says that she only wants log lines after she makes the request. "I'll ask for log lines. Rarely do I ask for a synopsis. If I like the log line, I'll reply with an attached submission form."

Nowak also strongly suggests that you do not send all of your log lines at once, especially if you have a lot of screenplays. "Don't let producers know you've got ten scripts, or whatever. They'll wonder why you haven't sold something yet."

GETTING A RESPONSE

Even if you get a "no thanks," continue to query when you have something that you feel they would be interested in. For example, I contacted a major independent production company and got a response from a secretary who informed me that they "do not accept unsolicited material" — you know, the usual. I e-mailed her back, thanked her for responding, and politely asked if there was anyone who would read my script. Sometimes the people most interested in reading are the ones not officially doing it, like secretaries. She asked to read it and eventually passed it on. (Everyone in Hollywood thinks they can be a producer.)

Opening a line of communication can sometimes be the difference between getting your first break or not. Don't ever be afraid to ask the question. After all, the worst they can do is say no.

Here's an example of a response from one of my e-mail queries:

> *Dear Chris,*
>
> *Thank you for your submission inquiry. Please follow up with a short paragraph(s) or log line(s) describing what your screenplay(s) is about.*
>
> *If we are interested in seeing the material, we will e-mail back our submission form with our address. If you do not receive a response, the material does not meet our current development needs. Please feel free to send other inquiry e-mails for any future projects.*
>
> *Sincerely,*
> *Mr. Big*

This company must get a fair share of e-mail, as this appeared to be a form letter that was sent out in response to my query. Notice that they requested a "short paragraph or log line." If they're interested, I will hear back; if they're not, I won't. Simple enough. So I crossed my fingers and sent them my best log line. I received this response:

Chris,

Thank you for your query. The attachment is our submission/release form. Please read, sign, and enclose with submission.

Thanks for sending us your screenplay for consideration.

Feel free to e-mail to check the status at: development@directnet.com. Please keep in mind we will not return scripts unless a self-addressed, stamped envelope is enclosed with your submission.

Scripts not under consideration are recycled.

This is one of the best responses I could hope to get. Not only do they request the screenplay, they offer an open door for contacting them, as I can e-mail to check the status of my submission.

There, I've passed the first test. If I can write a professional and well-crafted query, log line, or synopsis, chances are I might be a decent writer and the company I'm contacting will often respond.

THE OUTCOME

After mailing off your screenplay, give them two weeks, then e-mail to verify it was received. Wait another five to six weeks. By then, hopefully, you'll get a call, and it'll be good news.[1] If not, e-mail concerning its status. You should get a response that offers a specific explanation as to why you have not heard from them. It would not be good news if they offer no real information on the status of your screenplay. I'd give them

---

[1] If you have found this company or person through a directory or Web site, they should offer some instructions on how to submit to them, a time frame for getting back to you, and other information. They may even provide a form that you can fill out on their site.

another two weeks and e-mail a final time. Keep your e-mails short when inquiring about the status of your script (like one or two sentences). If they give you a runaround, it's time to move on. The fact of the matter is this: If they're really interested in your screenplay, they will call you. Good news never comes from the mailman, and the same goes for e-mail. They will call if they're really hot for your screenplay, to be sure.[2] (Note: Agents will sometimes send a letter requesting your script in response to written queries; sometimes they will call.)

FINAL THOUGHTS

One thing to avoid is mass querying. It's easy to send out thirty to forty e-mails in a couple of days. I recommend resisting this temptation. Be patient. What you'll find when you mass query is that your quality goes down significantly from number one to number thirty or forty.

The one time I mass e-mailed, I got a lot of responses but had a hard time keeping track of who was who. An even bigger problem I had was finding time to write my log lines, synopses, and treatments.[3] When you get a response from a producer, e-mail back as soon as possible. If it takes you a week to get back to them, you're old news. Keep your number of queries to around ten a week; that's plenty. Of those ten, you will hopefully get three or four responses. Plus always count on a few returned to you from your e-mail server. Producers and agents change e-mail addresses a lot, especially when they start getting sixty or seventy messages a day.

Avoid sending out your script when it's not ready to be seen. (It's the "patience thing" again.) A script that is not ready to be seen can just kill you — especially in today's Internet world where script coverage can change hands very quickly and easily.[4] You could ruin your chances with that producer or agent for good, as well as many others. Hopefully you

---

[2] Remember to document every correspondence in your portfolio.
[3] For more information on how to write a synopsis or treatment, see my website: *http://www.screenwritersutopia.com.*
[4] Even though it is against WGA rules, smaller companies sometimes have to resort to faxing and e-mailing each other script coverage to keep up with the big studios who have stables of readers. There are also message boards on the Web that are hidden, and are a gathering place for movie executives to discuss the various projects floating around from studio to studio. See "Top Secret! Development Hell on the Web," by Brendan Bernhard, *LA Weekly* at *http://www.laweekly.com/*

belong to a screenwriters group and can have other experienced writers read your screenplay and give you feedback. A good script alone is not enough. Have your log lines or premise statements completely developed. You should have log lines memorized for each script. Also have a well-written one-page synopsis prepared and your pitch well thought out. If all of these are completed and your screenplay is as good as you can make it, then start querying. Remember, you should have two or three screenplays that are ready to show before you start querying producers or agents. Sometimes they'll ask for more than one from you.

Finally, always save your rejection letters. Whenever possible, have an attorney review anything you sign, even release forms. If an independent producer buys or options your screenplay, they will really try to get it made. They do not option material unless they are extremely serious about it. They simply do not have the money to throw around. Signing with an agent or optioning a screenplay to an independent producer could just be that foot in the door you always wanted. Ouch!

CHAPTER FIVE

AGENTS & AGENCIES

The spec-script boom of the late 80s and early 90s is responsible for the lively "spec market" that exists today. "Up until the mid-eighties, the thrust of writing a script was more a calling card. They weren't the high concept that they came to be in the late eighties and early nineties," says Thom Taylor, author of *The Big Deal: Hollywood's Million-Dollar Spec Market*. "Writing a spec was a way to get into the business, get meetings, and get hired essentially. The studios would have the projects they wanted to do, and they would simply hire a writer to do it."

The spec boom lead to the creation of what is known as "tracking." It is the responsibility of development people working within a company to know who is writing what, and what material is hot. Though this still mainly concerns only the top writers, you can bet that if your script starts to generate some heat, it will be tracked.

A good agent residing at a reputable company is your best shot at generating major heat for your script, though as an unknown writer you should never limit yourself to just seeking an agent. You should simultaneously be pitching producers and production companies you find online. (See the next chapter.)

Literary agents represent not just writers, but actors, directors, and some producers. A full-service agency handles all of the above. A WGA signatory agent or agency is not allowed to take more than 10% of the earnings they procure for you. You'll also find that some of the bigger agencies will try to package their own talent together on hot projects.

Once a writer has signed, the agency (or agent) then develops a strategy for who will get the script and when. In the hands of a crafty agent, this process will start generating heat for your script. If it is conveniently leaked that, say, Frederick Levy is getting a script for Marty Katz, then you'll have trackers from other competing companies wanting in on the action as well. Remember, no one wants to miss out on the next great script.

Signing with a major agency gets you on the fast track quicker than any-thing else. However, finding an agent willing to read your screenplay, let alone take you on as a client, will be your hardest sell of all. It's what they call a "Catch-22." You need an agent to submit your script to the bigger companies, yet most of the good agents won't talk to you. They only want to hear from writers who will make them money now. "It is true that very few agents place a premium on finding or grooming writers," says professional screenwriter and author Ron Suppa. "Most agents want writers who will work and generate fees."[1]

One of the best spec screenplays to hit Hollywood in the 1990s was Andrew Kevin Walker's *Se7en*. With a script as good as his, you would think all he had to do was write up a couple of query letters and he would have his pick of major agencies. After many attempts he was unable to get even one agent to respond to his query letter. He then saw the movie *Bad Influence*, which he really liked, so he decided to contact its screenwriter, David Koepp. Walker wrote Koepp a very professional and meaningful letter asking that he read his script. Koepp, who was not accustomed to reading unknown writers' material, saw something in the letter that made him want to read the script. He did and eventually passed it on to his agent. And that's how Walker did it. His approach was the road less traveled, and a very bold one at that. But even with an agent, the script still languished for years before it was made.[2]

"I'm not an advocate of sending a hundred blind queries thinking that you're going to get their attention," says Thom Taylor, "because you're not, unless you had some success that can separate you from the pack."

You may have been told at one of those expensive seminars or classes that your spec script is your calling card. Just keep in mind that you're really nothing special, as there are about 20,000 other writers out there with the exact same credentials.

---

[1] Ron Suppa, *This Business of Screenwriting: How To Protect Yourself As A Screenwriter*. Los Angeles: Lone Eagle Publishing Company, LLC, 1999, 78.
[2] Thom Taylor. *The Big Deal: Hollywood's Million-Dollar Spec Script Market*. New York: William Morrow, 1999, 94.

As an aspiring screenwriter with nothing but a spec script to offer, be prepared to send out a couple of hundred query letters just to get a handful of responses. When you've made your first sale to a smaller company or producer, won or placed in a screenwriting contest, or obtained your first independent film credit, then use that as your calling card.

Even with credits, you'll find that doors won't just open by themselves. I have spoken with produced writers and directors of independent films who have found it difficult to break in with a major agency. If proven talent can't even find an audience among the top agencies, imagine how hard it will be for an unknown. Does that mean you shouldn't try? No, of course not. What I am proposing is this: Find the agents and agencies looking for new material — and it's no coincidence that you're going to find many of them online. Signing with a small, hungry agency could be very important and make all the difference for an aspiring screenwriter like you.

The Bewares Board! — *www.absolutewrite.com/forum/index.html*
Before you query any agent, you might want to check out this board. Writers can list agencies, publishers, and producers with whom they have had bad dealings. From the site: "In a perfect world, there would be no need for this board. Unfortunately... we haven't reached that stage yet. Writers, this is the place to post and read warnings from fellow writers." This board is moderated by Jenna Glatzer.

AGENTS LISTINGS

A.E.I. Online
Contact: Chi-Li Wong
9601 Wilshire Blvd
Box 1202, Beverly Hills, CA 90210
(213) 932-0407
Web address: *www.lainet.com/~aeikja/*
E-mail: *aeikja@lainet.com*

Comments: It's hard to call A.E.I., established in 1996, a "small" agency because they are quickly becoming a significant player in Hollywood. A.E.I. founder Ken Atchity has made millions of dollars for his clients. The best-selling author of *MEG*, Steven Alton, is one of his many successful clients. It's very easy to contact Vice President of Development Chi-Li Wong at the e-mail address listed above. She'll respond if they are interested in your query. They represent upwards of fifty writers, including authors and screenwriters. They always consider new talent.

Their Web site offers good information for writers and background on A.E.I., including what their current needs are. For submission guidelines, consult their Web site.

Aardvark Literary
3908 Harlem Rd., Suite 104L
Amherst, NY 14226
(716) 834-750
E-mail: *aardvark@localnet.com*

Comments: They represent books and screenplays. From time to time they take on new writers, and they are open to e-mail queries.

Cedar Grove Agency
P.O. Box 1692
Issaquah, WA 98027
Web address: *www.freeyellow.com/members/cedargrove/index.html*
E-mail: *CedarGroveAgency@juno.com*

Comments: They accept submissions in the form of a one-page synopsis for full-length feature films and MOWs. At the time of this writing, they are not interested in "horror, period pieces, or erotic thrillers."

Chadwick & Gros Literary Agency
Contact: Tony Seigan, Associate Editor and Overseas Officer
Lessman@Screenplay Pkwy 671
Baton Rouge, LA 70806
(225) 338-9861
Web address: *www.colorpro.com/chadwick-gros*
E-mail: *ChadGros@aol.com, agentAP@e-mail.com*

Comments: They have been servicing screenwriters since 1942 and are headed by Anna Piazza, who came to them from Rinehart & Associates, where she was a talent scout. When you send them an e-mail query, they expect you to be "brief and to the point. Include NOTHING of your work in the body of a letter, or as an attachment unless invited to do so."

Client First Agency
Contact: Robin Swensen
P.O. Box 128049
Nashville, TN 37212
(615) 463-2388
Web address: *www.nashville.net/~c1/client1.html*
E-mail: *cl@nashville.net*

Comments: Established in 1990, they represent novelists, screenwriters, interactive-software writers, and songwriters. They are primarily interested in published or produced writers; however, they will consider new writers. E-mail query is acceptable. They are a WGA signatory and currently represent more than twenty writers.

Dale Harney Productions
10737 St. Gabriel School Road NW
Edmonton, Alberta, T6A 3S7 Canada
(403) 463-3079
E-mail: *dhprod@planet.eon.net*

nments: Strictly for Canadian writers. They accept e-mail queries and do consider new writers.

Douroux & Co.
445 South Beverly Drive
Suite 310
Beverly Hills, CA 90212
Web Address: *www.relaypoint.net/~douroux/*
E-mail: *douroux@relaypoint.net*

Comments: As a signatory with the WGA (Writers Guild of America) and the DGA (Directors Guild of America), Michael E. Douroux has been a fairly successful agent for over fifteen years, working with both screen-writers and authors. They only consider established writers, but I think they're worth a shot. You can submit a query via a form on their Web site.

Feigen/Parent Literary Management
10158 Hollow Glen Circle
Bel Air, CA 90077
(310) 271-0606
E-mail: *104063.3247@compuserve.com*

Comments: Brenda Feigen is a Harvard Law School graduate and acts as "lawyer-agent," which means she charges her fee for legal services when requested and appropriate. Joanne Parrent is a published author, and produced screenwriter. They accept e-mail and letter queries from new writers. At any one time, they represent forty or more writers, including authors.

First Look Talent and Literary Agency
Contact: Burt Avalone
511 Avenue of the Americas
Suite 3000
New York, NY 10011
(212) 216-9522
Web Address: *www.firstlookagency.com*
E-mail: *FirstLookNY@firstlookagency.com*

<u>Comments</u>: Established in 1997 by Bert Avalone, Ken Richards, and Harry Noland, First Look has solidified itself as an up-and-coming agency. Their client base runs around twenty, and they usually sell a half dozen projects each year. They are open to e-mail queries but prefer you use a form they have provided on their Web site. They are open to new writers as well, and are always on the lookout for fresh and innovative material.

A Franc Group
2745 Jefferson, #B
Carlsbad, CA 92008-1742
(760) 720-2268
Web address: *home.sprynet.com/sprynet/ant1*
E-mail: *ant1@sprynet.com*

<u>Comments</u>: Send them a one-page synopsis along with your bio. Make sure to keep it fairly short. They will get back to you if they're interested.

Gloria Stern Agency
12535 Chandler Boulevard, #3
North Hollywood, CA 91607
(818) 508-6296
Web address: *www.hollywoodnet.com/Stern/index.html*
E-mail: *cywrite@juno.com*

<u>Comments</u>: She is an author and consultant who has connections in Hollywood. Give her a try.

Harris Literary Agency
P.O. Box 6023
San Diego, CA 92166
(619) 697-0600
Web address: *www.harrisliterary.com*
E-mail: *Hlit@adnc.com, n@adnc.com*

<u>Comments</u>: They prefer e-mail queries — no phone calls. Do not send

them more than a couple of hundred words in your initial query. Consult their Web site for current guidelines before contacting them.

Kaplan-Stahler Agency
8383 Wilshire Boulevard, Suite 923
Beverly Hills, CA 90211-2408
(213) 653-4483
E-mail: *ksagency@aol.com*

Comments: Send a short synopsis (no more than one page) of your story via e-mail.

Cyd LeVin & Associates
Contact: Rob Gallagher
8919 Harrat Street, Suite 305
Los Angeles, CA 90069
(310) 271-6484
Web address: *robgallagher.freeservers.com*
E-mail: *DealmakerX@AOL.COM*

Comments: Rob Gallagher has been in the entertainment industry for some time, as a packaging agent and former development executive. He readily accepts e-mail queries, and each query should contain title, genre, author, contact information, log line, and a fifty-word synopsis. He has signed several clients who found him from his Web site. Recently he sold a big-budget action spec entitled *Smuggler's Moon* to Warner Bros.

Monteiro Rose Agency
Contact: Milissa Brockish
17514 Ventura Blvd, Suite 205
Encino, CA 91316
(818) 501-1177
Web address: *www.monteiro-rose.com*
E-mail: *monrose@ix.netcom.com*

<u>Comments</u>: For over fifteen years, Monteiro has represented live-action and animation writers for children's television, feature films, home video, and interactive media. The agency's driving force is its co-founder, Candy Monteiro. Her background is in the music industry, where she worked for *Billboard* magazine. In 1984, co-founder Fredda Rose met Candy when the two of them worked at the Sy Fischer Agency, a Los Angeles–based literary agency. Together they started Monteiro Rose in 1987. This is going to be a tough one to get into, but they are open to your contacting them by e-mail with any questions.

Owen Prell Literary Agency
3450 Sacramento Street, #432
San Francisco, CA 94118
(415) 380-9268
E-mail: *PrellLit@aol.com*

PMA Literary & Film Management, Inc.
132 West 22nd Street, 12th Floor
New York, NY 10010
(212) 929-1222
Web address: *www.pmalitfilm.com*
E-mail: *pmalitfilm@aol.com*

<u>Comments</u>: Established in 1975, PMA is a fairly large "small" agency representing 70–80 clients. When you get ready to submit, please consult their Web site for current guidelines. They do request that every query "include basic information about your project (title, premise, length), and a brief paragraph on your background and future goals."

If you have any doubts about this one, I highly recommend you check out their Client Listings. It's a very impressive group.

QED Group, LTD
P.O. Box 4043
Portland, ME 04101
(207) 780-1949
Web address: *members.aol.com/QEDCEO/index.html*
E-mail: *QEDCEO@aol.com*

Comments: The Web site was being updated at the time of this publication and no information was available. Check their Web site for
submission guidelines when it is back online.

Rogers Literary Agency
656 Las Casas Avenue
Pacific Palisades, CA 90272
Web address: *home.earthlink.net/~kathyrogers*
E-mail: *RogersLit@aol.com*

Comments: The agency will represent new and established writers of
both fiction and nonfiction.

Sister Mania Productions, Inc.
Contact: James Stringfield
916 Penn Street
Brackenridge, PA 15014
(412) 226-2964 ext. 12
Web address: *thebridge.com/ibb/smpi/home.html*
E-mail: *jims@thebridge.com*

Comments: They are a full-service literary agency. However, they also
develop, package, and produce film and television projects for most
major and large independent studios. They accept e-mail queries, and
they have a Web page with specific instructions for submitting a project
to them.

Susan Schulman Literary Agency
454 West 44th Street
New York, NY 10036
(212) 713-1633
E-mail: *Schulman@aol.com*

Comments: They will accept feature-film scripts, teleplays, and stage plays. They are also interested in fiction, nonfiction, self-help, psychology-wisdom, and business material. Query with an e-mail for current submission policy.

Talent Source
Contact: Michael L. Shortt
107 East Hall Street
Savannah, GA 31401
Web address: *www.talentsource.com/literary.html*
E-mail: *mshortt@ix.netcom.com*

Comments: Founded in 1990 by Michael Shortt, they are a WGA signatory with over sixty clients. They are always on the lookout for "character-driven comedies and dramas," and they list *There's Something About Mary*; *sex, lies, and videotape*; and *Sling Blade* as examples.

Victoria Allen Literary Agency
1489 Thousand Oaks Blvd., Suite #2
Thousand Oaks, CA 91360
(805) 494-8012
Web address: *www.valitagency.com*
E-mail: *allen@valitagency.com*

Comments: They are a new literary agency seeking clients. E-mail them for submission guidelines.

The Wolfe Agency
Contact: Harry Preston
Web address: *www.thewolfeagency.com*
E-mail: *info@thewolfeagency.com*

Comments: Alexandra Wolfe heads the agency and has over fifteen years of experience in the industry. The agency recently teamed up with veteran literary agent Harry Preston of Stanton & Associates, based in Dallas, and Susan Taylor, a literary agent based in the U.K.

The Wright Concept
Contact: Marcie Wright, Founder
1612 W. Olive, Suite 205
Burbank, CA 91506
(818) 954-8943
Web address: *www.wrightconcept.com*
E-mail: *mrwright@wrightconcept.com*

Comments: Founder Marcie Wright began her career in 1983 as a literary agent at the Dona Lee Davies Agency, representing television sitcom writers. Her company, as you might imagine, specializes in TV writers, but not exclusively. They also represent feature-film writers. Every so often, they list a "writer of the month" on their site, highlighting one of their own writers who has sold or optioned a script.

The Vines Agency — William Clark
111 West 16th Street, Suite 3A
New York, NY 10011
(212) 229-0158
Web address: *www.wmclark.com*
E-mail: *wcquery@wmclark.com*

Comments: William Clark is a veteran of the industry, having worked at the William Morris Agency. He is a member of the Association of Authors' Representatives and represents screenwriters as well. He'll usually request a synopsis, so have one ready. When you query via e-mail, you should also be prepared to present your bio information and an outline of your story. He'll respond if interested.

CHAPTER SIX

PRODUCERS & PRODUCTION COMPANIES

"I truly believe great material can come from anywhere," says Vice President of Development for Marty Katz Productions and author of *Hollywood 101*, Frederick Levy. More and more producers and production companies are wising up to the fact that good material can, and does, come from anywhere. "Good material does find a way," adds Thom Taylor. "It doesn't matter where you're from or who you are. If you have a hot script that has, as they say, 'legs,' it will walk on its own." The key is getting it read. Once you can do that, a great script will usually take care of the rest.

Before contacting any producer, you should keep in mind that producers are very busy people. They are working incredibly long hours, and they are, for the most part, extremely driven. They live, eat, and sleep movies and projects. They have to in order to succeed. "For people working in this business, it's really a lifestyle," adds Levy. "It's not a nine-to-five job. It's bigger than you or your career. You have to adapt to that." So when producers are late getting back to you or say they're too busy, take their word for it and contact them at a later time. Don't take it personally, and always be professional.

As an aspiring screenwriter — an unproduced and unproven one — you can still express confidence in yourself. And know this: The majority of the independent producers you'll run into online need you almost as much as you need them — almost. Every one of them is looking for that next "big project," and that means a script. And that means you, the screenwriter. You may have just written the next *American Beauty*, and they know it.

Though the great age of spec-sale bonanzas is over, "Hollywood continues to buy more and more spec scripts," says Howard Meibach, author of the *Spec Screenplay Sales Directory*. "The producers are looking towards the Internet for material — especially the newer producers and smaller production companies. They usually get material that has been shopped to death. The Internet can provide them with fresh material."[1] That is the key. The Internet is a great source for new material.

"We want material to be submitted to us first. We want the first look. That's the name of the game," adds indie producer Michael Grace. "We're not interested in anything that has been shopped everywhere."

SELLING WITHOUT AN AGENT

An agent isn't the only person who can sell your script. "When trying to break in, everyone wants an agent," says Thom Taylor. "With *While You Were Sleeping* (written by Fredric Lebow and Daniel Sullivan), a producer was the catalyst. You don't have to have an agent to sell."

A producer will option your script, attach himself to the project, and then take it to the big fish in the pond. With any luck, a studio or major production company will buy it. If you're smart enough to have an entertainment attorney review the option agreement, you've just made a lot of money.

For more on agents see Chapter Five.

ZERO-OPTIONS

On two occasions, I've been offered what is called a "zero-option" by independent producers. The "zero" stands for the amount of money you get. You're basically allowing a producer to shop the script for free; if the producer sells it, you get paid. As with any option agreement, there is a time frame involved. I must confess, I agreed to a zero-option once. I will never do it again. Here's how I look at it now: A producer without any money really isn't a producer at all.

---

[1] Kenna McHugh, "Interview with Howard Meibach," at: *screenwritersutopia.com/interviews/kenna_10.html.*

THE LISTINGS

What follows is a select listing of small to major independent companies that have a Web site and/or e-mail address. These are the companies you'll have the most luck in contacting. You will not find a listing for Miramax, New Line, or Paramount, and the reason is simple: They do not want to hear from you. There are a couple of major companies like Marty Katz Productions who are open to hearing from you, and they are listed.

However, here's a warning: Several of the companies listed here are brand-spanking new, and that means they are unknown entities, so you must be careful and always have your script copyrighted before sending it out. Keep copies of all correspondence. If and when you get to the contract stage, hire an attorney to review anything you sign. That will cost you some money, but it's well worth it.

Each listing offers something on the background of the company, a "snailmail" address, usually a contact person, and a phone number. Some listings also have tips for querying that company and a key URL to get you pointed in the right direction. Good luck!

100% Entertainment
Contact: Stanley Isaacs
200 North Larchmont Blvd.
Los Angeles, CA 90004
Web address: *www.100percentent.com*
E-mail: *100percent@iname.com*

Comments: Stanley Isaacs is a former literary agent turned screenwriter and producer. Mr. Isaacs is an experienced producer with three films to his credit. He formed 100% Entertainment in 1999. He produces not just his own material, but other writers' as well. The company prides itself as a production and management company, with seven films currently in development. As of this writing, they list *Megalodon* as their most current production.

Aarambh Productions, Inc.
Contact: Kiran Merchant
P.O. Box 3157
Astoria, NY 11103-0157
(718) 544-4525
Web address: *www.idoctor.com/gene/aframe.html*
E-mail: *AARAMBH@worldnet.att.net*

Comments: As a full-service production company of independent feature films, Aarambh currently has two films in preproduction. Unsolicited scripts are accepted upon the signing of a release form.

Query Tip: They request that you check their Web site for submission guidelines.

Alchemy Films
Contact: M. E. "Dusty" Garza
3866 Simmons Avenue
Riverside, CA 92505
(909) 588-1452
Web address: *www.linkline.com/alchemy*
E-mail: *garza@linkline.com, alchemy@linkline.com*

Comments: For Alchemy Films founder Dusty Garza, the rising tide of independent filmmaking has been a source of inspiration. Alchemy has been around for several years now and seems to be struggling to get many projects off the ground. Mr. Garza comes from a television background, having worked in the industry for many years. He is a two-time Emmy Award nominee. They currently have several projects in development.

A-List Pictures
Contact: Tracey Glynn, Development
8981 Sunset Blvd., Suite 311
West Hollywood, CA 90069
(310) 385-0951
Web address: *www.alistpictures.com*

Comments: You'll need Shockwave installed on your computer to view this site. As of this writing, their site was mostly under construction. Check back with their Web site for submission guidelines at a later time.

American Interactive Pictures
Contact: Bill Crow or Peter Maris
40308 Greenwood Way
Oakhurst, CA 93644
(209) 642-0791
Web address: *www.aipictures.com*
E-mail: *bc@aipictures.com*

Comments: They are always interested in e-mail queries as to possible employment opportunities they may have. They specialize in motion picture, video, and CD-ROM production. They are more than likely *not* looking for stories, but writers. Query via e-mail for submission guidelines.

American Zoetrope Studios
5225 Wilshire Blvd., Suite 204
Los Angeles, CA 90036
(323) 935-5776
Web address: *www.zoetrope.com*
Key URL: *www.zoetrope.com/join.cgi*

Comments: A true sign of the times: One of our most celebrated directors, and one of the most established studios, has a major presence online. Francis Ford Coppola's company accepts submissions from writers on their site. There is a process, and it takes some time, but it costs you absolutely nothing.

Query Tip: Once you join, which is free, you'll receive a password. Once inside, you can access the "Zoetrope Virtual Studio" for screenplays. In order for your screenplay to be considered, you must first read and review four other screenplays by other writers. Your screenplay will then be read and reviewed. The highest-scoring screenplays are then read by Zoetrope. From there, the writer will be contacted if a producer likes something.

113

Past credits for Zoetrope include: *The Godfather, Apocalypse Now, The Legend of Sleepy Hollow, The Virgin Suicides*, and many others.

A.M. Productions/Qwato Interactive Studios
Contact: Scott Frost
6509 Lignum Street
Springfield, VA 22150
Web address: *www.amfilm.com*
Key URL: *www.amfilm.com/contact.html*
E-mail: *sideout@atlantatech.net*

Comments: Formerly known as A.M. Productions, Qwato Interactive Studios has developed into a film and interactive entertainment production company located in Virginia. They produce independent features, interactive games, and Web sites. They still have the same leadership, as president Scott Frost has been with A.M. Productions since its inception in 1985.

"We are truly excited about the opportunities this facelift will bring," says Frost. "It is the dawning of a new era in storytelling, and we feel that we have the talent to become a major player."

They list numerous credits, including *Shadow Zone, The Dark Side*, and *Enraged*, among others. Current projects include: *Awaken*, a CD-ROM game, and *A Good Man*, described as a "psychological drama." Visit their Web site for future submission guidelines.

Amphion Productions
Contact: Sara Coover Caldwell, Producer/Writer
Web address: *www.amphionpro.com/welcome.html*
E-mail: *info@amphionpro.com*

Comments: Writer/producer Sara C. Caldwell established Amphion Productions in Chicago in 1991 as an independent film and video production company. In 1997, she took the logical step of moving her company to Los Angeles. Her goal is to create films and documentaries "that entertain, educate, inspire, and touch audiences." They offer mostly writing services. At the time of this printing, they list *Crawl Space* as their most recent project in development.

Animas Pictures
Contact: Erik Burke, Writer/Director
835 Main Avenue, Suite 201
Durango, CO 81301
(800) 201-6890
(970) 385-8686
Web address: *www.animaspictures.com*
E-mail: *info@animaspictures.com, erikburke@animaspictures.com*

Comments: Mainly a film and video production and postproduction company, but they are looking to do more documentaries and feature films. They recently completed their first feature film, *The Loser.* Company president Erik Burke has over fifteen years of experience as a producer, writer, director, and cinematographer working in both New York and Los Angeles.

Arc Angel Films
Contact: Mark Witherspoon-Cross
1000 Universal Studios Plaza
Orlando, FL 32819
(407) 224-5506
Web address: *www.arcfilms.com*
E-mail: *mark@arcfilms.com, queries@arcfilms.com*

Comments: Located in Orlando, Florida on the back lot of Universal, Arc Angel was founded in 1997 mainly as a TV production company. They have since expanded into motion pictures as well. The principals are Mark Witherspoon-Cross, Howard Kazanjian, Rick Helmick, and Rhonda Witherspoon-Cross. Together they blend a nice mix of experience and knowledge of the industry. They list among their current projects *Shadows* (TV) and a feature film entitled *Claus.*

Query Tip: Check Web site for current needs and submission guidelines.

Ashley Productions
Contact: Development
5225 Canyon Crest Drive, #71-340
Riverside, CA 92507-6628
Web address: *www.ashleyproductions.com*
E-mail: *development@ashleyproductions.com;, projects@ashleyproductions.com*

Comments: Founded in 1997 by Jacqueline and William Ashley, Ashley Productions is located in Riverside, California. Jacqueline Ashley is the creative force, while William Ashley handles the business end. As an independent film production company, they are always on the lookout for that next great script. They list *Between Friends* as their only project currently in development. At my last check with them they are actively searching for shorts and features for production.

Query Tip: According to the site, "We look for good material that is uniquely distinctive. After all, film is forever. Not only is it an immortalization of those in front of the camera, but those behind it, as well. It is a body of work for everyone involved in its creation. Aspiring to be the best, we measure success not by the quantity of work, but by its quality."

Atlantic Streamline
Contact: Vanessa Coifman, Vice President of Development
1323-A Third Street
Santa Monica, CA 90401
(310) 319-9366
Web address: *www.atlanticstreamline.com*
E-mail: *info@atlanticstreamline.com*

Comments: They describe themselves as an "innovative" company with a goal to "develop and produce new talent." Those words are music to the ears of aspiring screenwriters everywhere.

Query Tip: Credits include the popular sci-fi film *The Thirteenth Floor*, and the crime/thriller *You're Dead*. They are one of the more innovative and original independent companies making feature films. For possible submission, e-mail Vanessa Coifman. You may need an agent to submit to them.

Avatar Films
Contact: Robin Lim, Acquisitions
121 West 19th Street, Suite 9-D
New York, NY 10011
Web address: *www.avatarfilms.com*
E-mail: *avatarfilm@aol.com*

Comments: Established in the summer of 1999, Avatar has produced three films, most recently the award-winning *Nico and Dani*. According to the site, their mission is "to bring films of a certain caliber and transcendence to a much deserved audience."

Bad Kitty Films
Contact: Sandra J. Hall, Acquisitions Manager
2431 Mission Street
San Francisco, CA 94110
(415) 642-MEOW (6369)
Web address: *www.badkittyfilms.com*
E-mail: *query@badkittyfilms.com*
Key URL: *www.badkittyfilms.com/Pitch_this.htm*

Comments: As a San Francisco–based, woman-owned, independent film production company, Bad Kitty prides itself as an innovative and professional organization "with lots of good karma." Founded in 1997 by executive producer Kimber O'Neill, an entertainment industry professional with over a decade of experience, their credits include *Jane, Appetite, 120 @ 2000, Jackpot, Once the Fog Rolls In*, and *Cat And Mouse*.

Query Tip: They manage and run an annual screenwriting competition that is a consistent source of material. They have optioned and developed over a half dozen screenplays from their competition. As an independent company, they are always on the lookout for "budget-conscious dramas or comedies." They willingly accept e-mail queries and encourage writers to enter their competition. They recently started a new service on the site that allows writers to pitch their story ideas to them online (see Key URL). It takes only a few minutes.

Big Dog Entertainment — Harbor Entertainment, INC.
Contact: Marlowe R. Walker, CEO
100A Gary Way
Ronkonkoma, NY 11779
(631) 738-1010
Web address: *www.bigdogpictures.com*
E-mail: *mwalker@bigdogent.com*

Comments: Big Dog Entertainment is a part of Harbor Entertainment, which also includes Stapleton Studios. Harbor Entertainment buys scripts and other properties to co-develop with other studios. Their most current project in development is an espionage thriller called *Puppet Man*.

Query Tip: As of this writing, they have already purchased the rights to many novels, short stories, and scripts by award-winning author Warren Murphy. This could be a legit possibility for the right writer. They are seeking "scripts that feature high action sequences and adventure motifs."

Bigel/Mailer Films
Contact: Daniel Bigel, Michael Mailer, or Chris Connolly
443 Greenwich Street, Suite 3A
New York, NY 10013
(212) 343-7916
Web address: *www.bigelmailer.com*
E-mail: *dbigel@bigelmailer.com*

Comments: This is the exact type of company you want to contact. As an independent company, Bigel/Mailer has a reputation for making excellent "small" films. Their credits include *Black and White*, *Two Girls and a Guy*, and the recently completed *The Last Producer*, directed by Burt Reynolds, who also stars. They have several films in development. Bigel/Mailer was formed in 1995 by its principals and executive producers, Daniel Bigel and Michael Mailer.

Query Tip: Check their site often for more information. They are seeking "strong and compelling stories." You might need an agent or referral to submit.

Blue Rider Pictures
Contact: Jeff Geoffray or Walter Josten
2800 28th Street, Suite 105
Santa Monica, CA 90405
(310) 314-8246
Web address: *www.blueriderpictures.com*
E-mail: *geoffray@compuserve.com*

Comments: Since 1991, Blue Rider has established itself as a solid independent film company producing quality films. They are best known for their film *Slow Burn*, a psychological thriller starring Minnie Driver (*Good Will Hunting*), who plays a young woman searching for treasure in the Mexican desert. Other credits include *Cord, My Five Wives, Silver Wolf*, and others. The principals of the company are Jeff Geoffray and Walter Josten.

Bodega Bay Products, Inc.
Contact: Michael Murphy, Producer
P.O. Box 17338
Beverly Hills, CA 90209
(310) 273-3157
Web address: *www.bodegabay.net*
E-mail: *bodegabay@msn.com, jp-bodegabay@msn.com*

Comments: This independent company produces not only motion pictures and television programs, but has moved into large-format (IMAX) film-making as well. They list *The Last Best Sunday* as their most recent project.

Bottom Line Studios
Contact: Patrick Donahue
(408) 806-2129
Web address: *www.bottomlinestudios.com*
E-mail: *bottln@mindspring.com*

Comments: Producers of low-budget "B" movie features including *Shattered Dreams, Ground Rules, Parole Violators*, and several others.

Query Tip: At the time of this printing, they are looking for martial arts action scripts with humor.

Braun Entertainment Group, Inc.
Contact: Sonia Apodaca-Harms, Director of Development
280 S. Beverly Drive, Suite 500
Beverly Hills, CA 90212
(310) 888-7727
Web address: *www.braunentertainmentgroup.com*
Key URL: *members.aol.com/braunent/submissions.htm*
E-mail: *SoniaAH@aol.com; BraunEnt@aol.com*

Comments: As of this writing, production just wrapped for their latest feature film, *Edges of the Lord* (starring Haley Joel Osment and Willem Dafoe). They have several projects in development. Principals Zev Braun and Philip Krupp are industry veterans with solid credits.

Query Tip: They are looking for "feature films, one-hour dramas, and MOWs. We are especially interested in true life, true crime, and stories in general with strong characters." They are not interested in stories with gratuitous sex and violence; also stay clear of "campy horror." If you do not have an attorney or agent, you will be required to sign a release form. This is obviously an excellent opportunity for any writer.

Broadbay Media
Contact: Stephen A. Madigan
823 Galloway Street
Pacific Palisades, CA 90272
(310) 573-0344
Web address: *www.broadbay.com*
E-mail: *steve@broadbay.com*

Comments: The company was founded in 1996 during what they describe as the "digital revolution." They develop material for feature films, television, and the Internet.

BroadMind Entertainment

Contact: Jennifer Marquis, Development
8530 Wilshire Blvd., Suite 404
Beverly Hills, CA 90211
(310) 855-8687
Web address: *www.broadmindent.com*
Key URL: *www.broadmindent.com/awards2000.html*
E-mail: *jen@broadmindent.com*

Comments: From their Web site, "BroadMind Entertainment (BME),
a Los Angeles–based film and television production company, seeks to
expand the scope of mainstream cinema by recognizing, developing, and
producing film scripts with distinctive and challenging screen roles for
both women and minorities."

Query Tip: The best way to get in the door here is to enter your screenplay in the *Cynosure Screenwriting Awards* competition (see Key URL
above).

Buffalo Gal Pictures

Contact: Lorne MacPherson, Liz Jarvis, Shawn Watson, or Josy Perciballi,
Producers.
777-70 Arthur Street
Winnipeg, Manitoba, R3B 1G 7 Canada
Web address: *www.buffalogalpictures.mb.ca*
E-mail: *bgal@mts.net*

Comments: Based in Winnipeg, Buffalo Gal Pictures is a Canadian
independent production company that produces motion pictures, short
films, documentaries, and music videos. Their most recent films include
The Law of Enclosures, *Desire*, and *Children of My Heart*.

Query Tip: Past projects have been mostly dramas with young-adult
and children themes. However, recently they did make a psychological
thriller. Query for current needs and guidelines.

Caine Entertainment
Contact: Julian Caine, Director and Chief Executive Officer
P.O. Box 1740
Studio City, CA 91614
(213) 304-8447
Web address: *www.caineentertainment.com*
Key URL: *www.caineentertainment.com/submissions.htm*
E-mail: *Development@CaineEntertainment.com*

Comments: President Julian Caine was an accountant, but not just any ordinary one. He has worked for MGM, Universal, and several other production companies. Mr. Caine is very ambitious and, at least, has the business know-how to make a company successful. The only question is, can he find the right material? This is a new company, but one worth a shot.

Query Tip: Consult their submission page at the Key URL listed above.

Cambium Entertainment
Contact: Development
18 Dupont Street
Toronto, Ontario, M5R 1V2 Canada
(416) 964-8750
Web address: *www.cambiumentertainment.com*
E-mail: *annette@cambiumentertainment.com*

Comments: Cambium Entertainment specializes in MOWs, animation, and television.

Query Tip: They deal mostly with family programming in a variety of formats and media.

CLC Productions
Contact: Development
1223 Wilshire Blvd., Suite 404
Santa Monica, CA 90048
(310) 246-9388
Web address: *www.cathylee.com/clc.htm*
Key URL: *www.cathylee.com/mail.htm*
E-mail: *cathylee@cathylee.com, development@cathyleee.com*

Comments: Cathy Lee Crosby's company does buy scripts. The Web site heavily promotes her book and movies, so don't be fooled. She has several projects in development: *The Orpheus Conspiracy, The First Earth Battalion, The Gift of Chance, Blue Moon* (written by Jeff Arch, *Sleepless in Seattle*), and *Cloud's Cradle*. She stars in and co-produces all of her films. This is a legit opportunity.

Query Tip: If you have a story that has a strong female character over the age of 35, then contact her company.

Code 3 Productions
Contact: Development
4055 Tujunga Ave., Suite #111
Studio City, CA 91604
(818) 766-9044
Web address: *www.code-3.com*
E-mail: *development@code-3.com, mail@code-1.com*

Comments: They list one current project titled *Heaven Up*. A couple of years ago they were heavily advertising on their site seeking scripts. They have since toned that down. E-mail for submission guidelines.

Creative Leisure Group
Contact: Gary Stamford, Producer
2101 Chambers Street
Victoria, BC, V8T 3L1 Canada
(250) 382-9922
(250) 415-2922

In the United States:

P.O. Box 1825
El Segundo, CA 90245
(310) 299-7860
Web address: *members.tripod.com/clgroup*
Key URL: *members.tripod.com/clgroup/submit.html*
E-mail: *clgroup@bigfoot.com, clgroup@fastmail.ca*

Comments: Creative Leisure Group is a West Coast–based operation located in both California and British Columbia. On their Web site, they list *Rocks* as their only credit.

Query Tip: They are currently seeking "low-budget horror… the next *Breakfast Club*." They are also on the lookout for "erotic thrillers."

Crimson Pictures
Contact: Bryan Darling, David Corby, Producers/Directors
Web address: *www.crimsonpictures.com*
Key URL: *www.crimsonpictures.com/submitinfo.html*
E-mail: *bryan@crimsonpictures.com, david@crimsonpictures.com*

Comments: A very small independent film production company, they specialize in video and multimedia and, in the past, have focused on music videos. They have four feature films in various stages of production.

Query Tip: Visit Web site (Key URL) for current needs and submission guidelines.

Crown International Pictures
Contact: Development
8701 Wilshire Blvd.
Beverly Hills, CA 90211
(310) 657-6700
Website address: *www.crownintlpictures.com*
E-mail: *crown@crownintlpictures.com*

Comments: From their Web site: "Over 40 years as a leading force in Independent film production and distribution to the worldwide entertainment industry, with a library of over 110 feature films for theatrical, television and video distribution."

Cypress Films

Contact: Jon Glascoe, or Joseph Pierson
630 Ninth Ave., Suite 415
New York, NY 10036
Web address: *www.cypressfilms.com*
Key URL: *www.cypressfilms.com/submissions.html*
E-mail: *lovisa@cypressfilms.com*

Comments: Over the past twelve years, company principals Jon Glascoe and Joseph Pierson have produced many popular and award-winning television programs and films in several countries. Cypress Films is an independent New York–based production company, founded in 1987. As for credits, they recently produced *Nuremberg*, one of the most watched miniseries ever on cable. They also have about a half dozen other films to their credit, going back to 1988.

Query Tip: They would generally like your agent to contact them, but are willing to take e-mail queries via the Key URL link listed above. From the submission page: "Send us a BRIEF e-mail describing your completed screenplay; we may ask to read the actual script. And unless you say something truly frightening, we always reply courteously. And remember: we are an independent film production company, which means that your screenplay about alien invaders blowing up New York will not find a home here." They have several films in development — several dramas, and a true-story adaptation. They are generally interested in films that can be made in the $1–2 million range.

Dark Horse Entertainment

Contact: Development
100 Universal City Plaza, Bldg. 507-3F
Universal City, CA 91608
(818) 777-5830
Web address: *www.dhorse.com*
E-mail: *development@dhorse.com*

125

<u>Comments</u>: Founder Mike Richardson established Dark Horse Entertainment in 1992. The company's first two major films were big hits: *The Mask*, starring Jim Carrey and Cameron Diaz, and *TimeCop*, starring Jean-Claude Van Damme. Most recently they produced *Mystery Men*. Currently in development, they have *Concrete*, based on a character created by Paul Chadwick.

Query Tip: If you haven't noticed, this company specializes in comic-book heros.

Destiny Pictures
Contact: Mark Castaldo
11718 Barrington Court, Suite 411
Los Angeles, CA 90049
(310) 440-0409
E-mail: *destinypictures@hotmail.com*

<u>Comments</u>: Producer Mark Castaldo's credits include *The Perfect Tenant* and *The Perfect Nanny*. Destiny Pictures has been in business for more than three years now. They have several films in development, including *The Woodpecker Waltz*, dealing with the death penalty. They request e-mail queries only.

Query Tip: "I am always looking for a good thriller, in the vein of *The Hand That Rocks The Cradle*," says Castaldo. As for your e-mail query, Castaldo asks, "Keep the synopsis short; some people get long-winded and send 2–3 pages. Ten lines at the most should encompass what I need to know."

Devin Entertainment
Contact: Gregory H. Sims, CEO
1888 Century Park East, Suite 912
Los Angeles, CA 90067
(310) 557-3660
Web address: *www.devinintl.com*
E-mail: *devin@devinintl.com*

<u>Comments</u>: Devin is committed to producing and distributing films that are artistically diverse and have the potential to be monetarily successful. They have numerous credits and several films in development. Their credits include *Blackmail, The Fear 2: Halloween Night*, and others.

Dream Ribbon Productions
Contact: Gregory Bennett, Creative Director
(416) 421-6875
Web address: *www.dreamribbon.com/drp_welc.html*
E-mail: *info@dreamribbon.com*

<u>Comments</u>: Based in Toronto, Ontario, Canada, they specialize in film, video, and Internet productions for the business community as well as developing and producing original films and videos. They list *Children of the Shadows*, a documentary, as their most current project.

Delta Blue Productions
Contact: Development
Web address: *www.maxpages.com/deltablue*
E-mail: *deltabluemedia@yahoo.com; deltablue@rubyridge.com*

<u>Comments</u>: As an international network of independent filmmakers, Delta Blue Productions is currently seeking scripts. Current projects in development include *Nouvelle Western, A Cowgirl Legend, The Sandbox*, and *An American Family*.

Query Tip: They will accept e-mail synopses of no more than one page.

DIC Entertainment
303 N. Glenoaks Blvd.
Burbank, CA 91502
(818) 955-5400
E-mail: *dicmikeg@aol.com*

<u>Comments</u>: They deal mainly in television, animation, and interactive multimedia. Credits include *Where in the World is Carmen San Diego, Inspector Gadget*, and others.

127

Digital Arcana, Inc.
Contact: Jeffrey Sullivan, or Bruce Onder
3211 Fernwood Avenue
Los Angeles, CA 90039-3510
(213) 964-6121
Web address: *www.digitalarcana.com*
E-mail: *jas@DigitalArcana.com; bonder@DigitalArcana.com*

Comments: Digital Arcana writes, designs, and produces award-winning CD-ROM and online games such as *Command & Conquer*. Query via e-mail, but you should have some interactive writing background.

Dimitri Villard Productions
Contact: Dimitri Villard, President, Sisan Danforth, Development
8721 Santa Monica Blvd, Suite 100
Los Angeles, CA 90069-4511
(310) 229-4545
E-mail: *dvillard@loop.com*

Comments: Credits and projects include *Timewalker, Death of an Angel, Once Bitten, Flight of the Navigator*, and *Purgatory*.

Emerald Oceans Entertainment
Contact: Quinn Katz, Vice President of Development
Web address: *www.unsigned.cc/maint/script.cfm*
Key URL: *www.unsigned.cc/maint/script2.cfm*
E-mail: *quinn@eomedia.com*

Comments: They produce mainly low-budget screenplays of all genres. They list *Raising The Stakes* as their most recent credit.

Query Tip: You can query them online from a submission form (Key URL). "If you are interested in submitting a screenplay for consideration or just interested in getting more information in general, please visit the site."

The Farnham Film Company
Contact: Development
34 Burnt Hill Rd.
Lower Bourne, Farnham, Surrey, GU10 3LZ, U.K.
+44 (0)1252 710313
Web address: *www.farnfilm.com*
E-mail: *info@farnfilm.com*

Comments: They will consider projects by new writers. They are not looking for big-budget action films; they are an independent company looking for quality drama. Query for current needs and submission guidelines.

Film Kitchen
Contact: Doug Lindeman
P.O. Box 40
Hermosa Beach, CA 90254
Web address: *www.filmkitchen.com*
E-mail: *info@filmkitchen.com*

Comments: They have an impressive list of small independent film credits, some award-winning. Accomplished writer/director Kirk Harris heads the company and writes most of their movies. Doug Lindeman is an L.A.-based producer and co-owner of the respected publicity firm Cottrell-Lindeman and Associates.

Query Tip: Visit Web site for possible submission opportunities. All of their productions have been under $1 million.

Filmworld, Inc.
Contact: Development
4929 Wilshire Blvd., Suite 830
Los Angeles, CA 90010
(323) 954-0377
Web address: *www.filmworldinc.com*
E-mail: *info@filmworldinc.com, fworld@filmworldinc.com*

Comments: In 1999, Filmworld was formed by Menahem Golan, one of the more successful filmmakers in the motion picture industry. He has worked on such films as *Superman*, *A Cry In The Dark*, *Delta Force*, and many others. Filmworld's first project was *Death Game*, written by Timothy White and starring Sean Young. Current projects include *Elian*, about the Gonzales boy who was found off the Florida Keys in a raft after his mother died trying to gain their freedom from Cuba in 1999. They have numerous projects in development.

Query Tip: All of their productions have been suspense thrillers or action pictures.

FilmSaavy Entertainment
Contact: Craig Saavedra
16931 Dearborn Street
Northridge, CA 91343
Web address: *www.filmsaavy.saavedra.com*
E-mail: *FilmSaavy@aol.com*

Comments: Craig Saavedra has already done some quality work, and in a relatively short period of time. As a former Hollywood tour guide turned filmmaker, his films have won awards and gained recognition. His past credits include the highly acclaimed *Rhapsody in Bloom*, starring Penelope Ann Miller and Ron Silver.

Query Tip: Check their site for possible submission opportunities.

First Look Pictures/Overseas Filmgroup
Contact: Development
8800 Sunset Blvd., 3rd Floor
Los Angeles, CA 90069
(310) 855-1199
Web address: *www.ofg.com*
E-mail: *info@ofg.com*

Comments: First Look Pictures is a division of the Overseas Film-group, established in 1993 to package, finance, and distribute motion pictures in the U.S. They acquire projects at virtually any stage, from development to postproduction. They do have an acquisition and development department, which may be worth a look, especially if you have a finished film. They list several films currently in production, including *Skins* starring Graham Greene and Adam Beach, *Young Blades*, and *My Kingdom*.

Flying Rhino Productions, Inc.
Contact: Development
500 Tamal Plaza, Suite 520
Corte Madera, CA 94925
Web address: *www.flying-rhino.com*
E-mail: *Info@Flying-Rhino.com*

Comments: They specialize in 3-D animation, film and video productions, and multimedia.

Girlie Girl Productions
Contact: Lisabeth Laiken, Assistant Producer
1520 North Vista Street, Suite 203
Los Angeles, CA 90046-7900
(323) 851-1206
Web address: *www.girliegirlproductions.com*
Key URL: *members.telocity.com/~owenville/sub.html*
E-mail: *info@girliegirlproductions.com*

Comments: President Elizabeth Owen and producer Kimberlyn Marie Lucken are the principals. Both come from development and production backgrounds.

Query Tip: They are looking for "Story, story, story. It goes without saying (or at least it should) that every story needs a beginning, a middle, and an end. That doesn't mean, of course, that they need necessarily go in that order (*Pulp Fiction* anyone?) but there must be something cohesive

131

there, or it won't be of interest to us." Submit a professional query, and they will contact you if they are interested in reading your script. Check their Web site (Key URL) for more guidelines.

Given Films

Contact: Daniela Soto-Taplin, Producer
28 Warren Street
New York, NY 10007
(212) 962-9375
Web address: *www.givenfilms.com*
E-mail: *dsoto60@hotmail.com*

Comments: Founded by Harvard dropout Galt Niederhoffer in 1996, Given has produced eight films including *Hurricane Streets*, released by MGM in 1998. The film won Best Director, Best Cinematographer, and the Audience Award at the 1997 Sundance Film Festival. I think this is a great opportunity. They list *Intern* as their most recently completed project at the time of this writing, which also made it to Sundance 2000.

Grade A Entertainment

Contact: Andy Cohen
368 N. La Cienega Blvd.
Los Angeles, CA 90048
(310) 440-0409
E-mail: *GradeAProd@aol.com*

Comments: Andy was a producer and development executive for a number of companies, including Norman Lear's Act III Productions (*Fried Green Tomatoes*), Permut Presentations (*Face/Off*), and Orr and Cruickshank Productions (*Father of the Bride, Sister Act*). He started Grade A in 1996 and has produced such films as *Billboard Dad, A Chance of Snow*, and *It Takes Two*.

Query Tip: They only accept e-mail queries, no phone calls, and according to Andy, "All writers are welcome to send us an e-mail with a short synopsis about their finished work." Also, Andy has seen too many writers attach files to their e-mail, which he will not open and certainly will not read. He *does* like it when writers can "be brief and are to the point. Sell us on your material. If your script sounds like a strong, well-written, commercial idea, chances are we'll want to take a look."

Green Communications

Contact: Development
303 N. Glenoaks Blvd., Suite 605
Burbank, CA 91502
(818) 557-0050
Web address: *www.greenfilms.com*
E-mail: *info@greenfilms.com*

Comments: Founded in 1990 by Talaat Captan (President), Green Communications has quickly emerged as one of the leading independent film companies. They produce and distribute, which is a major advantage for them but also an indication that they have grown into a major independent company. As of this writing, they list *The Time of Her Time*, as their most recent film. Past projects include *The Blood of Others*, which starred Jodie Foster.

Groovy Entertainment

Contact: Eirik Tyrihjel
Web address: *www.groovyentertainment.com/english/index.html*
E-mail: *eirik@groovyentertainment.com*

Comments: For the past three years, Groovy Entertainment has serviced the Norwegian market, mainly producing commercials, music videos, a few short films, and a feature film. In 1997 they made their first feature film, which lost money. They seem very enthusiastic. Keep an eye on this one for possible future submissions.

Gruenberg Films

Contact: Andreas Gruenberg
Blankenburger Chaussee 84
D-13125 Berlin, Germany
phone/fax: +49(0)30-94 32 999
Web address: *www.gruenbergfilm.com*
E-mail: *Andreas.Gruenberg@gruenbergfilm.de*
Key URL: *www.gruenbergfilm.com/needs.htm*

Comments: As a European company that gets most of its financial back-
ing from European investors, your best action/adventure script would
be a good bet here. But keep in mind that their budgets are in the $3- to
$20-million range. Their credits include *Poison*, a dark thriller starring
Rosanna Arquette. They list scripts recently optioned, and several are
by English/American writers.

Query Tip: They are looking for feature-film and MOW scripts in all
genres, but check their "Needs" link (Key URL) for changes. Every
three months or so, they have a new "Call for Entries." According to
the site, "We will consider all genres except for sci-fi and horror. There
is particular interest in thrillers, action/adventures, romantic and black
comedies, and dramas."

Guerilla Films

Contact: David Nicholas Wilkinson
35 Thornbury Road
Isleworth, London TW7 4LQ England
+ 44 (0)20 8758 1716
Web address: *www.guerilla-films.com*
E-mail: *david@guerilla-films.com*

Comments: Since 1996, this company has had a presence on the Web.
They are a small independent film production and distribution company
based in London, England, run by David Nicholas Wilkinson. Credits
include *Seaview Knights*, Michael Radford's *Another Time, Another Place*,
and the award-winning *The Perfect Circle*. They are happy to hear from
new writers; e-mail query of course. Visit Web site for current submission
guidelines.

Hyperion Studio
Contact: Development
111 North Maryland Ave., Suite 300
Glendale, CA 91206
(818) 244-4704
Web address: *www.hyperion-studio.com*
E-mail: *administrator@hyperionpictures.com, hyperion@hyperion-studio.com*

Comments: Hyperion Studio specializes in young-adult and family-oriented live-action and animated feature films and television. Their film credits include *Playing By Heart* and *Tom's Midnight Garden*.

Jumprope Productions
Contact: Chris Emerson
10932 Morrison Street, #108
Studio City, CA 91601
Web address: *www.jumpropeprods.com*
E-mail: *submission@jumpropeprods.com*

Comments: Jumprope Productions was formed in 1999 by producer Chris Emerson. Their goal is to discover and build relationships with new talent.

Query Tip: At the time of this writing, they have an open-door policy to new writers with new material. They are currently looking for "conceptually driven material to develop and produce." They have several projects in development. They do not want phone calls; only e-mail queries to the address above.

Marty Katz Productions
Contact: Frederick Levy, Vice President of Development.
1250 6th Street, Suite 205
Santa Monica, CA 90401
Web address: *www.hollywood-101.com*
Key URL: *www.hollywood-101.com/lessonplan/resources/writers/martykatz.html*
E-mail: *HllyWd101@aol.com*

<u>Comments</u>: Marty Katz Productions has a first-look deal with Miramax and Dimension Films. Past credits include *Man Of The House*, *Lost In America*, *Mr. Wrong*, *Titanic*, and others.

Query Tip: First, read our interview with Frederick (Chapter Ten). As of this writing, they are interested in "sci-fi of the mind, along the lines of *Twilight Zone* as opposed to *Star Wars*. Horror, but not *Scream* — it's already been done. Something smart and new that stretches the genre. Thrillers, either action thrillers or psychological thrillers (*Se7en*); but they must have a hip edge. Low-budget urban comedies. Projects with a touch of class (*Life is Beautiful*, *Shakespeare in Love*)." For current needs and guidelines, visit Web site, Key URL.

Kingman Films International
801 North Brand Blvd., Suite 630
Glendale, CA 91203
(818) 548-3456
Web address: *www.kingmanfilms.com*
Key URL: *http://www.kingmanfilms.com/e-kasa/ekasal.htm*
E-mail: *info@kingmanfilms.com*

<u>Comments</u>: Kingman Films International is a young, innovative production and development company whose goal is to create "fresh, original feature films that combine commercial and artistic values to entertain and enlighten." I highly recommend their KASA million-dollar screenwriting contest, as that is how they select nearly all of their projects for production.

Query Tip: They now have what they call "e-pitch." See Key URL listed above. You can pitch your screenplay to them on this page in minutes.

Kline, Adam/Ark Pictures
Contact: Adam Kline
6423 Wilshire Blvd., 1st Floor
Los Angeles, CA 90048
Web address: *hollywoodnet.com/arkpix*
E-mail: *arkpix@aol.com*

Comments: Adam is always looking for good material. If you have a finished feature-length screenplay, then send, e-mail, or fax a five- to seven-sentence summary of one or more of your screenplays. The e-mail address listed above should connect you right to Adam himself. See my interview with Adam in Chapter Ten.

Eddie Kritzer Productions
Contact: Ms. Claire Wee, Executive Story Editor and Eddie Kritzer, Producer
8484 Wilshire Blvd, Suite 205
Beverly Hills, CA 90211
(323) 655-5696
Web address: *www.eddiekritzer.com*
Key URL: *www.eddiekritzer.com/query.htm*
E-mail: *info@eddiekritzer.com*

Comments: Eddie Kritzer has served as producer, creator, or consultant to such shows as *Kids Say the Darndest Things*, starring Bill Cosby and Art Linkletter, *Shattered — If Your Kid's On Drugs*, and many more.

Query Tip: Kritzer is actively seeking "compelling manuscripts and screenplays for immediate consideration." They prefer nonfiction and true stories, but will consider any genres that are of good quality.

Laughing Horse Films, Inc.
Contact: Cheryl Read
7777 10th Ave. SW
Seattle, WA 98106
(206) 762-5525
E-mail: *LHFILMS@aol.com*

Comments: Most recent projects include *The Actor*, which is directed by Martin Sheen and written by Pulitzer Prize–winning writer Jason Miller. They are only looking for material in the $2- to $4-million range. Contact Cheryl for needs and submission possibilities.

Leo Grillo Productions
Contact: Leo Grillo
P.O. Box 2
Acton, CA 93510
(323) 957-0062
Web address: *www.leogrilloproductions.com*
Key URL: *http://www.leogrilloproductions.com/screenform.htm*
E-mail: *lgrillo@earthlink.net*

Comments: Producer Leo Grillo has several films in production. His first produced credit was *Deirdre's Party*.

Query Tip: They have a submission page on their site for screenwriters (Key URL). Send log line with query.

Leviathan Pictures
Contact: Robert Duncan, Submissions Department
P.O. Box 5475
Riverside, CA 92517
Web address: *www.leviathanpictures.com*
E-mail: *rjduncan@leviathanpictures.com*

Comments: They welcome script submissions of all genres from screen and television writers. Agent submissions are not required. They do require a release form to be signed with all submissions.

Lucid Media, Inc.
Contact: Marino Colmano
7120 Alcove Ave.
North Hollywood, CA 91605
(818) 764-8580
Web address: *www.loop.com/~macbravo*
E-mail: *macbravo@loop.com*

Comments: As a producer, director, writer, editor, and cinematographer, Lucid Media's Marino Colmano has won over thirty international awards. He has worked for Castle Rock, TriStar, MGM, and Walt

Disney, as well as for television, including the hit show *M*A*S*H*. Lucid has several projects in development and is open to e-mail queries. But they do ask that you "please refrain from sending any e-mail attachments prior to sending a query e-mail."

Query Tip: Mr. Colmano seeks to produce material that is "provocative, intelligent, positive, and explores the human condition."

Malibu Entertainment
Contact: Stefano Esposito
270 N. Canon Dr., Suite 1236
Beverly Hills, CA 90210
(310) 226-7107
E-mail: *StefanoE@aol.com*

Comments: They accept screenplays only after a short e-mail query, and if they are interested they will send you a release form.

Malamute Entertainment
Contact: Donna Strader, Producer
3530 Shadow Walk Drive
Houston, TX 77082
(281) 597-8586
Web address: *www.malamute-entertainment.com*
Key URL: *www.malamute-entertainment.com/submissions/submissions.htm*
E-mail: *info@malamute.cc*

Comments: Based in Houston, Texas, they are an independent company with one official credit, *The Distinct Smell of Red*. From the site: "We work with the filmmaker to stay true to the original vision while keeping the project within the desired budget."

Query Tip: They have a submission page (Key URL) that outlines how to submit to them. They are a Texas-based company, and proud of it, as their Web site seems to cater to Texas filmmakers in general.

Mase/Kaplan Productions, Inc.
4001 W. Alameda Avenue, Suite 301
Burbank, CA 91505
(818) 557-2990
E-mail: *Akaplan@leondaro.net*

Comments: E-mail for submission guidelines and policy. Their credits
include *Red Shoe Diaries* (cable) and others.

Mindfire Entertainment
Contact: Ann Marie Kaesman, Director of Development; Mark Altman,
Producer
3740 Overland Avenue
Los Angeles, CA 90034
(310) 204-4481
Web address: *www.mindfireentertainment.com*
E-mail: *mkaesman@mindfireentertaiment.com*
       maltman@mindfireentertainment.com

Comments: Mindfire seeks to bring "a hip, independent sensibility to a
variety of movie genres." Their first film was the award-winning *Free
Enterprise*, followed by *The Specials*. They have several projects in development. Visit their Web site for current needs and submission guidelines.

Moher Films
Contact: Development
1803 W. Magnolia Blvd.
Burbank, CA 91506
(888) 440-8143
Web address: *www.moherfilms.com*
Key URL: *www.moherfilms.com/contest.htm*
E-mail: *development@moherfilms.com*

Comments: Founded in 1998, they seek to produce quality independent
films. Their current project slate includes both film and TV.

Query Tip: Moher Films is looking to establish a group of in-house writers. They accept queries via the e-mail address listed above. They also have a contest for screenwriters (Key URL). The winner will receive a $5,000 script option. The entry fee is $55.

New Amsterdam Entertainment, Inc.
Contact: Michael Messina, Director of Development; Richard P.
        Rubinstein, CEO
675 Third Avenue, Suite 2521
New York, NY 10017
(212) 922-1930
Web address: *home.att.net/~newamsterdamnyc/*
E-mail: *newamsterdamnyc@att.net*

Comments: You'll need to request a release form to sign before submitting. They just finished production on Frank Herbert's *Dune*, a sci-fi miniseries, and have several projects in development. Of note, they have optioned Lawrence Block's novel, *Hit Man*, to develop as a feature film.

No Prisoners
Contact: Development
2260 S. Centinela Avenue
Los Angeles, CA 90064
(310) 979-9097
Web address: *www.noprisoners.net*
E-mail: *info@noprisoners.net*

Comments: Founded in 1995 by entertainment executive and producer Todd Moyer, No Prisoners describes itself as a producer of "visually stimulating and adrenaline-rushing entertainment." Their first production was *Wing Commander*.

Outlaw Productions
Contact: Development
9155 Sunset Blvd.
West Hollywood, CA 90069
(310) 777-2000
Web address: *www.outlawfilm.com*
Key URL: *www.outlawfilm.com/contact_frame.html* (with e-mails to virtually everyone on the staff, including development)
E-mail: *outlaw@outlawfilm.com*

Comments: Producers Jeffrey Silver and Bobby Newmyer have made some pretty good films: *sex, lies, & videotape; Indian Summer; Three to Tango*; and many others.

Pirromount Pictures
Contact: Lee Neville
P.O. Box 7520
Van Nuys, CA 91405
Web address: *www.loop.com/~pirro*
E-mail: *pirro@loop.com, pirromount@msn.com*

Comments: At the time of this printing, they are not currently accepting submissions. Their current film is *Color Blinded*. Check their site for future submission possibilities.

Rage Entertainment
Contact: David Felder and Chris Daniel
P.O. Box 685
Neptune, NJ 07753
Web address: *www.ragefilms.com*
Key URL: *www.ragefilms.com/rage5.htm*
E-mail: *rage@ryanvideo.com, dpcdvideo@aol.com*

Comments: They are seeking "comedies, horror, or suspense films," low-budget scripts with a limited number of locations and speaking roles. They currently have a six-month backlog and ask that you be patient about a response. They list *Lady Dracula* as their most current project in development.

Redeemable Features
Contact: Development
381 Park Avenue South
Penthouse
New York, NY 10016
(212) 685-8585
Web address: *www.redeemable.com*
Key URL: *www.redeemable.com/contact.htm*
E-mail: *info@redeemable.com*

Comments: Their credits include *All I Wanna Do* (*www.alliwannado.com*) and *The Dream Catcher*, among others. They list *Center of the World* as their most recent project. Their site is excellent and offers some great information with a little humor.

Query Tip: "If you are not represented or are not sleeping with a member of our company, you can mail, fax or e-mail a one-page brief of the project you wish to submit." Now that's what I call an open-door policy! Their submission page (Key URL) has a release form that can be printed out if they request your script.

Ridini Entertainment Corp.
Raleigh Studios
650 N. Bronson Avenue
Los Angeles, CA 90004

&

534 Broad Hollow Road, Suite 430
Melville, NY 11747
Web address: *www.ridinientertainment.com/proddiv.htm*
E-mail: *RidiniFilm@ridinientertainment.com*

Comments: They are actively involved in the acquisition, development, packaging, financing, production, and sale of properties for motion pictures, television, and the Internet. They are interested in "setting up co-productions and joint venture projects ONLY IF a project has partial financing and/or star cast attachments." They list several films to their credit, including *Falling Fire, Future Fear, Convict 762,* and several others. They request that inquiries be kept short.

River City Productions
Contact: Brian Cutler, Director
Web address: *www.actorsstudio.com/rivercity.htm*
E-mail: *bjcutler@actorsstudio.com*

Comments: River City Productions, a division of The Commercial Actors Studio in Kansas City, is run by former-actor-turned-director, Brian Cutler.

Query Tip: As of this writing, they are interested in "any style, any length, any budget!" This is a new company with no credits.

Ro Sham Bo Productions
Contact: Development
Web address: *www.roshamboproductions.com*
E-mail: *admin@roshamboproductions.com*

Comments: They have a release form on their site that must be sent in with submissions. They are looking for low-budget scripts with a good story and nudity! (A good combination, according to them.)

ScriptStar Pictures
Contact: Michael Grace
P.O. Box 3364
Warrenton, VA 20186
Web address: *www.scriptstar.com*
Key URL: *www.scriptstar.com/writers.htm*
E-mail: *mgg@scriptstar.com*

Comments: A new company (March, 2000) started by Chris and Michael Grace, they are looking to make medium-budget, feature-length motion pictures. They are ready to go once they find the right project. "The financing is already in place; we can move rapidly once a suitable project is located," says Michael Grace.

Query Tip: "We want material to be submitted to us first. We want the first look. That's the name of the game. We want to get ahold of the fresh material." See Key URL for more information. Also, see my interview with Michael Grace in Chapter Ten.

Shoreline Pictures
Contact: Morris Ruskin
1901 Avenue of the Stars, Suite 1800
Los Angeles, CA 90067
(310) 551-2060
Web address: *www.shorelineentertainment.com*
E-mail: *shoreline@shorelineentertainment.com*
   mail@shorelineentertainment.com
   shoreline_90067@yahoo.com

Comments: In 1994, Shoreline co-founder Morris Ruskin co-produced *Glengarry Glen Ross*. Recent credits include *The Godson, Matter of Trust, Bug Buster, Detour, Clubland, The King's Guard, The Visit, Flight of Fancy,* and *The Big Twist*. They are an in-house production company.

Simon Tse Productions, Inc.
Contact: Jill Nowak, Director of Development
9060 Santa Monica Blvd. #106
Los Angeles, CA 90069
(310) 385-9331
E-mail: *stpwest@earthlink.net*

Comments: As a small production company, they produce features in the $1- to $2-million range. They list *Fatal Blade* as their most recent credit.

Query Tip: "We're always looking for action and thriller material — not much comedy, which is hard to sell in the overseas markets. I do enjoy horror but haven't had much [come] in that I liked. Not big on big epics; we're a small company," says Nowak.

Smash Alley Film Productions
Contact: C. Thomas Vasiloff
3 The Carriage Way
Thornhill, Ontario, L3T 4V1 Canada
(905) 886-3196
Web address: *www.nextlevel.com/smash*
E-mail: *smash@aracnet.net*

Comments: They claim to be the most aggressive film company in Canada. They accept queries via e-mail. Current projects include *Streets of Rage, Conspiracy of Brothers*, and *One Step Over The Edge*.

Square One Productions
P.O. Box 8332
Portland, OR
(503) 294-0934
Web address: *www.teleport.com/~sqarzvil/index.html*
E-mail: *sqarzvil@teleport.com*

Comments: They specialize in short films, documentaries, and corporate films. Query for submission policy and current needs.

SteppinStone Entertainment
Contact: Julie Avola
P.O. Box 8417
Universal City, CA 91618
(818) 766-0123
Web address: *www.steppinstone.com*
E-mail: *kantoku@primenet.com*

Comments: Since 1990, King Wilder and Julie Avola have helmed this company as an independent. They do not offer much information on their site, and I could only find one film credit: *Predators from Beyond Neptune*. Check their Web site (which is cool, by the way) for future submission possibilities.

Take 3 Film Productions Ltd.
Contact: Alan Kool/Mark Hartwell
350 Richmond Street, Unit #3
London, Ontario, N6A 5N9 Canada
(519) 675-1938
Web address: *www.take3films.com*
E-mail: *take3@take3films.com*

Comments: Their current projects include *Cry Of Silence* and *Ninagi*. Visit their Web site, and query by e-mail for submission possibilities.

Telescene Film Group Inc.
Contact: Anita Simand, Head of Creative Affairs
5705 Ferrier Street, Suite 200
Montréal, Québec, H4P 1N3 Canada
(514) 737-5512
Web address: *www.telescene.ca*
Key URL: *www.telescene.ca/html/team.html*
E-mail: *asimand@telescene.ca*

Comments: Telescene does just about everything: "Movies of the week, features, and television series." Writers who contact them will have better luck if they are represented.

Query Tip: They are looking for "high-quality" writing that plays to a "global market."

Terence Michael/Finney Productions
Contact: Terence Michael Producer, or Richard Finney, Writer/Producer
264 S. La Cienega Blvd., Suite 131
Beverly Hills, CA 90211
(310) 201-0700
Web address: *www.terencemichael.com/mfp.html*
E-mail: *linktm@earthlink.net*

Comments: Terence Michael began his professional career at Warner Bros. after hopping the fence and knocking on a door, which turned out to lead to the office of *Lethal Weapon* director Richard Donner. Miraculously, Terence wasn't kicked off the lot. Instead, Mr. Donner sent him down the hall to his wife's office, where he was allowed to spend one summer as an intern for producer Lauren Shuler-Donner.

Since that time, Terence has produced high-quality, art-house feature films, including *If Lucy Fell*, which premiered at the Sundance Film Festival in 1996. In 1997, he produced *Fall*, which premiered at Slamdance before being distributed by MGM/Orion Pictures.

His most recent productions include *There's No Fish Food In Heaven*, *My Sweet Suicide*, *Peroxide Passion*, and *Baggage*. His company accepts e-mail queries and has done so for several years now. (For more information on Richard Finney, see my interview with him in Chapter Ten.)

Troma Films
Contact: Lloyd Kaufman, President
Troma Studios
Radio City Station
P.O. Box 486
New York, NY 10101
Web address: *www.troma.com*
E-mail: *tromacon@aol.com*

<u>Comments</u>: Got the next *Toxic Avenger* script? Great, burn it... no, wait — go ahead and send it to them. The e-mail address listed above is for the president, so why not pitch him your sickest idea for a movie?

TS Productions
Contact: Dave Rinson
PMB 265 50 Lexington Avenue
New York, NY 10010
E-mail: *dr8755@yahoo.com*

<u>Comments</u>: In their own words, "We're looking for anything that can be shot for under a million dollars in the New York City area. It's

important to us that the main characters be in their early thirties and that night exteriors are kept to a minimum." They are a new company with no major credits.

Vigilante Girl Films
Contact: Heather Fay, William Jensen, Co-founders
812 North Avenue, Suite 63
Los Angeles, CA 90042
Web address: *www.vigilantegirl.com*
Key URL: *www.vigilantegirl.com/vgmain.html*
E-mail: *heather@vigilantegirl.com*

Comments: A brand new company that claims to have excellent industry contacts and is in search of their first project. Heather Fay and William Jensen seem very hungry to make their new company work.

Query Tip: They say they "will read EVERYTHING" you send them, or at least they will for now. You must, however, sign their release form, which can be found on their Web site.

Warner Sisters Productions
Contact: Cass Warner, Harry M. Warner
5720 Valley Oak Drive
Los Angeles, CA 90068
Web address: *www.warnersisters.com*
E-mail: *warnersister@earthlink.net, president@warnersisters.com*

Comments: Their goal is to make "affirmative, more insightful, and uplifting pictures." Visit their Web site for more details and submission possibilities.

White Rock Film International & Rampage Films

White Rock Film International
2412 Columbia Street, 2nd Floor
Vancouver, BC, V5Y 3E6 Canada
(604) 684-8687
Web address: *www.whiterockfilm.com*
E-mail: *whiterock@whiterockfilm.com, gwilding@axione.com*

Comments: Rampage Films is an affiliated production company to White Rock Film International.

Query Tip: They are looking for "teen thriller, horror, or anything scary." They produce two films per year. They list several credits including *Stag, Convergence*, and *Christina's House*. Projects in the $2- to $4-million range only.

Michael Wiese Productions

Contact: Michael Wiese
11288 Ventura Blvd., Suite 821
Studio City, CA 91604
(818) 379-8799
Web address: *www.mwp.com/pages/aboutus.html*
E-mail: *mw@mwp.com*

Comments: Mr. Wiese recently finished co-directing *Field of Fish*, which premiered at the Raindance Film Festival in London. E-mail for possible submission opportunities.

Zeta Entertainment

Contact: Mark Yellen or Zane Levitt
8315 Beverly Blvd.
Los Angeles, CA 90048
(213) 653-4077
E-mail: *zetafilms@earthlink.net*

Comments: Credits include *The Big Squeeze, Shiloh, Guncrazy, Fist of the North Star*, and *One Good Turn*.

Zodiac Pictures International

Contact: Development
6715 Hollywood Blvd., Suite 200
Los Angeles, CA 90028
(323) 466-1800
Web address: *www.zodiacpictures.com*
Key URL: *www.zodiacpictures.com/contact/home.htm*
E-mail: *development@zodiacpictures.com*
    ukas@zodiacpictures.com
    markus@zodiacpictures.com

Comments: Producers Lukas Hobi and Markus Kaeppeli formed Zodiac to build a financial bridge between Hollywood and Europe. The overseas market is very important to Hollywood. Zodiac is trying to become a major part of that union. "ZPI develops original screenplays with writers in both Europe and the United States." They list *Exklusiv* and *Misguided Angels* as their only completed projects. They currently have several films in development.

Query Tip: They are looking for action, thriller, and comedy screenplays.

CHAPTER SEVEN

THE SCRIPT SITES

If contacting producers or agents directly isn't working for you, there are script sites, which have developed over the last couple of years. They provide writers with various services, sometimes for hefty fees, and they seek to provide an environment where seller and buyer can interact when they otherwise would not have the opportunity.

Way back when — in Internet time it's ages ago — I remember when a script site was nothing more than a Web page where you listed your name, contact information, log line, and maybe a synopsis. No hefty fees and no submission process or script coverage. Today they have become a serious business, and thousands of writers have already paid hundreds of dollars or more to submit their material. Along with the business aspect comes one major improvement: more hope for success.

"The Internet is a great way to find new material and to do so cheaply," says Script Shark co-founder Ed Kashiba. These sites have a realistic shot at becoming players in the industry because they can connect with more writers than any agent or agency would ever want to, and they can indeed do so fairly cheaply. Not only that, they can act as middlemen helping writers garner deals without agents.

There is a "slush pile" of material out there. What the script sites are attempting to do is make that material more readily available, and hopefully find the needle in the haystack. In 1999, Script Shark was the first script-coverage site founded by Hollywood development executives. Today, there are dozens of sites that have opened their doors. Nothing is required, only a completed script and some cash. You don't need an agent to submit to these sites, and no begging or pleading query letters.

Though the service they are providing writers is essentially a facilitation of what an agent or agency would do, the line they walk is ambiguous enough to avoid the laws and regulations that agents must follow. There are some sites that perform the exact same duties an agent would. Remember Karen from Chapter One? Storybay helped her option her screenplay and even helped her work out the deal, going over the contract with her line by line.

According to the California Labor Code, anyone who "charges, attempts to charge, or receives an advanced fee from an artist" is considered an agent and therefore required to be bonded and follow the rules and regulations that are designed to protect you and other artists from exploitation. Yet there is a significant difference between "advanced fee agents" and what most of these sites do. By providing script coverage some script sites become service providers, not agents. In a way it is a loophole for them to charge a fee in advance.[1]

Currently, there are no laws that prohibit or make it illegal for a script brokerage site to charge writers or even to take a finder's fee or back-end fee (a percentage) if a writer sells a script from their site. The big risk with the Web is the lack of regulation.[2]

But look closely at the Web, and I think you'll find that if the information or service is valuable, you will have to pay for it. If a company can really get your script read by an industry professional reader, and help you connect with agents and producers, then that should be worth something to you.

WHAT THEY DO

Script sites do one or all of three things:

One: *coverage*. The writer gets a basic critique of a script by someone who is supposed to be a professional reader. Coverage is intended to determine the quality of the script. "The coverage reports we generated were just a by-product in our search mechanism for new talent and projects," Kashiba explains.

---

[1] Ben Berkowitz, "Sell Script on Web? Well, the Odds Are Better Than Powerball," *inside.com*, 2000.
Web: *www.inside.com/jcs/Story?article id_6733&pod_id=10*
[2] Ibid.

Some coverage is fairly extensive and falls more under *analysis*, where specific elements of the story are broken down for the writer. Generally speaking, when your script is covered, you get a log line, synopsis, and a one-page critique of the story.

When your script is "recommended," the doors start to open, a little. "Those are the scripts we read immediately and often wind up buying," says one executive. "A 'consider' goes on top of my stack with a somewhat lesser priority. And if it comes back as a 'pass,' it's dead."

Two: *internetworking*. The opening up of lines of direct communication with the industry is crucial. Your coverage, if you wish, can be available for agents and producers to view. Whether via message boards, databases, or directories, the theory is that the Hollywood professional will find your listing and contact you. In some cases the writer may also contact potential buyers directly. Each of these sites lists companies who they claim visit regularly looking for new material.

Three: *guidance*. If your script is exceptional, the company will work with you to develop your story and arrange meetings and even representation. In the end, the hope is that a sale can be made.

FEE-BASED SERVICES

Here are a few of the major sites that charge a fee for their services. Most fee-based sites offer script coverage; some do not. It's important to know exactly what you're getting for your money.

Script Shark — *scriptshark.com*
Founded in August 1999, Script Shark was the first online screenplay-coverage company created by Hollywood development executives. With the sole purpose of searching out new talent and material, and doing so cost-effectively, Script Shark is well ahead in the game. In February 2000, *ifilm.com* acquired Script Shark, which significantly solidified it not only economically, but commercially as well. Is Script Shark making money? "Absolutely, [but] we're not making money off of

the submission fees. The way we do make money is from subscriber fees from industry clients," says Kashiba. "The Internet is a great way to find new projects from a completely new source." Industry professionals can use Script Shark to find new material and, according to Kashiba, they have hundreds of members doing just that.

Quote from the site

"Script Shark's team of analysts are top professional readers actively reading for many of the companies listed below. Professional readers are required to work in complete confidence between companies."

What they do

You submit your material to them. They read, analyze, and write up a coverage report. This report will then place your material in one of three categories: RECOMMEND, CONSIDER, or PASS. They will send you the coverage report.

If your material receives a RECOMMEND analysis, they will call you to set up a meeting with an agent in L.A. to begin preparations for submitting your material to studios and/or production companies whom they list in their "Industry Contacts" section.

A CONSIDER analysis means you can post an abbreviated form of your coverage on their Spec Market site free of charge. They claim that this area is visited by industry professionals on a daily basis. Script Shark has a staff of twenty to twenty-five readers who perform the coverage for them. And best of all, "It's a requirement for us that they are working readers," adds Kashiba.

A PASS means nothing happens. You do get a copy of the coverage report.

Script Shark has also started a new service called "Story Notes," which provides writers with a complete analysis of the screenplay as opposed to coverage. "It was basically because a few of our readers (who are, or used to be, development executives doing notes all of the time) really wanted to try and help out these writers," Kashiba told me.

Doing more script analysis really places Script Shark ahead of most script sites. By giving writers an in-depth look at the strengths and weaknesses of their screenplays, Script Shark can help them prepare for their script to be covered. The only hang-up is that most writers will not be able to afford the hefty fee.

What it costs

Screenplay coverage (under 150 pages) $155
They will not accept screenplays over 150 pages.

Manuscript coverage (under 350 pages) $250
If over 350 pages, add $10 for every 50-page increment above 350 pages.

Story Notes (under 140 pages) $300
Five to eight pages of in-depth analysis of your screenplay.

Success stories

As mentioned before, Mark L. Smith, in early 2001, sold his spec script *The Devil's Kiss* to Icon (Mel Gibson's company) and Paramount for a low six figures. They have had several other success stories as well. Producer Greg Silverman discovered Craig Doyle and helped him to get an agent and is developing his project. "He has a well-written script," Silverman says, "And here is a guy I would have never had any contact with if it wasn't for Script Shark."[3]

Writers Script Network — *writersscriptnetwork.com*
If it were a race, the Writers Script Network would be Carl Lewis and all the rest, well, a bunch of nobodies. Founder Jerrol LeBaron has created the most successful script site on the Internet. As a former construction company and jewelry business owner, without any entertainment business background, Jerrol hardly seems like the person you would pick to be so successful at this business. "I think that helped me get a better perspective on everything," says LeBaron. "There are so many do's and don'ts and I didn't get filled up with all those negative pieces of information that

---

[3] Josh Chetwynd, "Filmmakers getting discovered online," *USA Today*, June 7, 2000.
Web: *www.usatoday.com/life/cyber/tech/cth709.htm*

someone with that kind of background might have. It allowed me to have a really fresh perspective on the business."

A fresh perspective might be the key, but what probably made the most difference was the research that was put into the site. "I did a lot of research and found a common ground and I didn't have any preconceived notions. We interviewed almost 200 agents, managers, and producers. I operate the site as a business. I didn't just throw it together. If you look at the successful dot-coms, they approached it in the exact same way."

Quote from the site

"Our initial research indicated that over 150 production companies use the Internet to find scripts, with more than 25% of these companies boasting good to excellent film credits. Since that time, the figure has greatly increased and Writers Script Network, by itself, has more than 700 registered industry members who now have access to writers' scripts."

What they do

Of all the script sites, the Writers Script Network is not trying to do as much, and therefore is able to focus on one thing alone: helping the producer easily find a good script. They offer no script coverage or notes. The site features an extremely diverse and powerful database that allows its users to quickly and efficiently find the exact type of material they are seeking. You the writer pay a small fee (per script) to post the title, log line, description, synopsis, treatment, and even the full script for each work in their database. The key to all this is accessibility and efficiency, and by far the Writers Script Network is perfecting it. They have more agents, managers, producers, and production companies using their site than anyone else, and that is why they are succeeding.

What it costs

To place your script and pitch, and to gain access to other information in their database, costs $30 per work.

Success stories

The site launched on Valentine's day, 2000, and since then they have helped a staggering amount of writers sell, option, and find representation. In the last twelve months, fourteen full-length scripts and seven screenplay shorts have either been sold or optioned via the Writers Script Network. This is not including the three writers who have found work, and another forty-eight writers who have gained representation. "You've got reputable *agencies* who can't do that!" boasts LeBaron.

You may see all the names of these lucky individuals on their site, and if you have any questions, or wish to contact them, simply send the Writers Script Network e-mail.

Storybay — *storybay.com*

The creators of the infamous script-coverage site *gocoverage.com* are the same people behind Storybay. *Gocoverage.com* sold script coverage to development executives, and even posted the coverage in a secure database online. The scripts they covered consisted mainly of spec scripts that were being shopped around town by an agent or agency. All this was done without the writers' consent. What was wrong with the idea was that bad script coverage could ruin a writer's chances with other companies, so you can imagine how screenwriters and their agents felt about the site. It lasted only a week before it was forced to close its doors.

Storybay.com is co-founder Brad Warrington's attempt at taking the road well traveled, which is usually a safe bet. The only problem is that this time they are well behind in the game, which means clearing the air in terms of what they are trying to accomplish with this new Web site. "*Gocoverage.com* was a completely different business," Warrington has said. "We developed Storybay based on the feedback we got from executives, the agencies, and writers. Storybay now focuses on the new writer."[4]

---

[4] As quoted from *www.storybay.com* in reference to a *Variety* article, "*Gocoverage.com* creators return online revamped." September 29, 2000. Web: *www.variety.com*

What they do

Storybay still does script coverage; however, this time it is available only if the writer agrees. It is their mission to increase the number of buyers, including agents and managers, to which writers are exposed. And this means providing buyers with efficient, legally safe access to an extended selection of material that would otherwise not be available.

Your script is given a "market analysis," which is fancy-speak for coverage. You can have a basic or extended analysis. Nothing happens if your script is not endorsed by them. If a script is endorsed, it will then be placed in their database. Once there, members can view your coverage and contact you if warranted.

If your script is highly regarded by Storybay, they can, in addition to listing you in the database, make what they call "direct presentations" to key industry buyers on your behalf in order to build a "fast buzz" for the script.

I also notice that there is an additional "7.5% success fee." This appears to be a back-end fee that would come into play if they sold or optioned your script.

Quote from the site

"Storybay is a service, which provides new, unrepresented writers the opportunity to rapidly get their work to the marketplace. It creates a level playing field for talent worldwide by offering unbiased professional feedback and direct access to buyers, as well as agents and managers."

What it costs

For one- to two-page coverage, the cost is $175.
Extended (five to ten pages) coverage is $300.

They also deal with manuscripts ($375), teleplays ($175), and treatments ($150).

Success stories

They have four listed on their site that I could find. Here's the most recent: In January Karen Kinsman, a fifty-year-old mother living in Perry, Maine, signed an option agreement for her first screenplay, *Tomorrow's Wish*, with Canada's Millbrook Productions (see Chapter One). The terms I received in a press statement said the amount was undisclosed, but that she would maintain some creative control and a piece of the back end. Not too bad.

Script P.I.M.P. — *scriptpimp.com*
"Pipeline Into Motion Pictures" is what the P.I.M.P. stands for. They match your script with the needs of production companies from their database. Every month, industry professionals visit the site and update the database with their current needs. All contacts are confidential, and material is only available upon request. Writers are notified when someone wants to read their scripts.

Unlike most of the other companies listed here, Script P.I.M.P. only deals with screenplays, which I think is a plus. They also accept electronic submissions, Final Draft format only, another plus. A credit card and a Final Draft copy of your script can have you signed up and submitted in minutes.

What they do

You do not have to pay for script coverage. You can pay a small fee to have your script "circulated" in their database where over 300 producers, directors, agents, and companies can find it. If you choose to have coverage done, they guarantee turnaround in 10–14 business days. Script coverage is kept confidential unless the writer wishes it to be available. Much like Script Shark, a script will receive a PASS, CONSIDER, or RECOMMEND. If your script is given a CONSIDER or RECOMMEND, Script P.I.M.P. will continue to provide notes for the writer until both parties feel the script is ready for circulation in the database. If a writer receives a PASS, he/she may rewrite the script and resubmit for an additional $60. They also take a back-end fee, or what they call a "finder's fee," if you sell your script on their site.

In early January 2001, Script P.I.M.P. formed an alliance with the Writers Script Network. What that means for you is that Writers Script Network will feature P.I.M.P.-recommended material within their database. (This is at no extra charge to the writer.)

Quote from the site

"Why we are supplying this service? Because, on a rainy night in January, we don't want you to be strolling by a romantic little restaurant on Main Street where John Cusack is dining with a beautiful starlet, and having you hustle two blocks home to your cramped studio by the beach to grab your script." And it goes on. The motto of the story: You may not have an agent, but you have something else... a pimp.

What it costs

Two- to three-page script coverage is $125.
Database circulation without coverage is $60.

Success stories

The lack of success stories on their site was a major disappointment. Not one could be found. "We are very young, nine months. Our biggest success story thus far is the positive feedback we continue to receive from writers. We strive to provide the best possible notes, and our writers have been thankful and very satisfied," says co-founder Chadwick Clough. "I've been working very hard, trying to help writers find their deserved niche in the marketplace — so hopefully we'll have a big success story soon."

NON-FEE-BASED

InZide — *inzide.com*
Hollywood producer Warren Zide's credits include such hits as *American Pie* and *Final Destination*. He launched *inzide.com* last September as a

means for helping unestablished writers submit their scripts to a real, and major, Hollywood company. Zide did not like what he considers to be a lot of unscrupulous online companies taking advantage of writers. "A lot of these places are like, 'Send in $200 and we'll get you a professional reader,'" says Warren. "What people do not realize is that it's just some out-of-work assistant in the back room doing the work." [5]

What they do

After reading and agreeing to their submission agreement, the writer can submit a two- or three-sentence log line to them. If they like the log line, they will request that you send the script. They prefer it be sent electronically. It must be sent in a script-program format. They support pretty much every program out there. It usually takes from two to eight weeks to hear back from them.

Quote from the site

"The staff at *inzide.com* will do their best to get back to you within a week after receiving your log line to let you know whether we are proceeding or not. Please be patient as it sometimes takes longer, but you will always get an answer one way or the other."

Success stories

They have reported optioning and developing several screenplays from their site.

Zoetrope — *zoetrope.com*

On September 8, 2000 Zoetrope announced that it had optioned two scripts from its Web site. If you're not familiar with *zoetrope.com*, you'll want to know that it is associated with Francis Ford Coppola's American Zoetrope production company. His credits include such classics as *The Godfather, The Conversation*, and *Apocalypse Now*, as well as recent hits like *The Rainmaker*.

---

[5] Ibid.

"We have always believed in the priority of finding new and excellent writers and stories. The advent of *Zoetrope: All-Story* magazine, and our new Zoetrope Studios virtual studio site, is beginning to give us a real advantage, as well as helping writers whose work might not otherwise be seen," says Coppola on his site.

How it works

You first read and review four screenplays by other writers. Then you can submit your screenplay, which is read and reviewed by four different writers. The ones that receive high marks are then passed on to Zoetrope for review.

Quote from the site

"American Zoetrope and other producers on this site will be reading the highest-scoring screenplays and may contact you to buy your story or hire your services. You may remove your story from consideration at any point."

Success stories

As I mentioned, they have optioned two scripts. As of this writing, there are over 12,000 writers who are members, with dozens signing up every day. Over 3,800 screenplays have been submitted for review so far.[6]

Hollywoodlitsales — *hollywoodlitsales.com*
Howard Meibach has created an outstanding resource for writers. Not just a script site, but a community where writers can read interviews and get script-sales and other valuable information, most of which is free. He is also author of the very successful book *The Spec Screenplays Sales Director*, which is now available on his site in a database. Howard has had a Web presence for some time and is well respected.

This site is now subsidized by Black and Blu Entertainment and the Steve Tisch Company, the people behind such films as *Forrest Gump, I Know What You Did Last Summer, Risky Business, Donnie Brasco,* and many others.

---

[6] Ibid.

What they do

Essentially you are submitting your log lines to them for consideration, and you can do so at no cost. But you are also submitting to a database that is organized by genre, type, keyword, and writer. Nothing is done without your permission. Industry professionals search through the listings at their leisure. Pretty simple, nothing really unique other than the important fact that you don't have to pay for it. They only accept material for feature films, cable, and network TV movies (MOWs) — no sitcoms or TV specials.

One possible hang-up: Anyone can sift through the log lines, which might be a problem for some.

Quote from the site

"Let the people at Sony-based Black & Blu Ent. and The Steve Tisch Co. as well as lots of other producers and agents know about your material." Sounds good!

Success stories

I know the site is actively used by development people from some major companies. They also reportedly have several writers who are working with Black and Blu developing their projects. Their biggest sale came when producer Ralph Macchio (*My Cousin Vinny*, *Can't Be Heaven*) bought *Forever Together* from the site. Kandu Entertainment has reportedly optioned a couple of screenplays from the site as well.

OTHER SCRIPT SITE RESOURCES
(both fee- and non-fee-based)

Studio Notes — *studionotes.com*
A new site, and one with an innovative approach, I think. Instead of offering script coverage for writers, they furnish development notes

from former development executives, not out-of-work readers. The cost is $300. Perhaps the biggest thing going for them is the site's founder, writer-producer Brent Armitage (*Gross Pointe Blank*). As a working writer and producer, he brings some legitimacy to the site, which is much needed.

It is also important to note that they do not take a finder's fee or back-end fee like some script sites, and they seem dedicated to the screenwriter. "A first-time writer makes what, $50,000 against $250,000 — if they're lucky — and you're going to take 10% ($5,000) from the guy. That's not right," says Armitage.

Your development notes will come from a former development executive with whom you can then have a consultation ($100 per hour), which is also something unique. "We offer solutions, not coverage that only points out the problems. We give a helping hand, and we will talk to you over the phone," added Armitage.

The only significant flaw I can see is the cost. It's a little steep for most writers.

Writers Website — *writerswebsite.com*
A free service that allows writers to post their material (a description or synopsis) and contact information for agents, producers, and the general public to review.

CinemaNow — *cinemanow.com*
You can submit your script to be included in a "virtual studio" they are building. CinemaNow is directly aligned with Trimark Pictures. The site is designed mainly for filmmakers.

Creative Script Services (CSS) — *thescript.com*
This is a unique site that offers management as well as script coverage. It is a fee-based service ($300). Of interest, they will also accept completed film submissions on a VHS tape. You get from three to five pages of notes with suggestions for improvement. They guarantee turnaround in

two to three weeks. The company is owned by Hollywood veteran Kathryn Knowlton, who has over fifteen years of experience working in the industry. She has a very impressive list of credits and credentials. CSS is worth a look.

Screenconnect — *screenconnect.com*
Their site provides professional evaluation for screenplays ($125) and manuscripts ($250). If it meets "certain criteria," they will list it in their database, where Hollywood producers and companies can find it.

The Script Agency — *thescriptagency.com*
Writers can submit a script for free, and they will apparently read it for no fee as well. If it receives high marks, they will "market" your script to their list of producers, development executives, agents, and managers who are working in the motion picture industry.

StoryXchange — *storyxchange.com*
A marketplace for writers of short stories, novels, poetry, and scripts. You can list your story in their "vault" for $9.95 per year, per story. For $99.95 you can get unlimited access. If you secure a sale via their site, there is also a back-end fee — 5% of the purchase price and/or option price.

The Spec Script Library — *thesource.com.au*
One of the original free script-posting services, founded in 1997. It currently lists over 2,200 scripts in its index. It claims to be the largest script index of its kind. You get to post a log line and contact information for every one of your scripts. They also list a "Scripts Wanted" section that unfortunately has only a dozen or so listings. At the time of this writing, they were in the middle of an overhaul.

TV-Pilot — *tv-pilot.com*
You can pitch your idea directly to the TV industry. You pay $30 per month to list your program ideas in their database.

My Movie Idea — *mymovieidea.com*
At *mymovieidea.com* you post your movie idea in 250 words or less. Every year, one idea will be chosen for development into a feature. They have apparently secured some kind of funding that will allow them to make the movie and fly the winning person to L.A. to receive $50,000. You can submit as many different ideas as you wish; there is no limit. However, there is a registration fee of $9.95 per idea. The site seemed to indicate this was a special offer, so the price may go up.

The Writing Zone — *thewritingzone.com*
They allow you to place your stories, novels, and screenplays online in their library of material. From the site: "A world where literary expression collides full force with the Internet." You can post your script for $9.95.

Script Cave — *scriptcave.com*
The Cave will take your script and get it into the hands of someone who might sign you as a client or buy your screenplay. Their Web site played some real hip and cool music, has lots of bells and whistles, the whole nine yards — just nothing seems legitimate. It was extremely annoying. At the time of this writing, their news section had nothing in the way of success stories, and the site appeared to be under construction. I do know that, at one time, they were charging $100 to cover scripts.

ScriptREADER — *scriptreader.com*
ScriptREADER is an analysis program that gives you coverage of your script. If you're really just looking for some good coverage, check out this site and save a ton of money.

THE GLOBAL MARKETPLACE

Script sites are setting out to create a global literary marketplace, one that can potentially help thousands of writers who would otherwise not have much of a chance at selling their scripts due to geographical barriers alone. A global market concept is certainly a worthy idea. Right now the Internet is only scattered with companies and producers seeking material.

It's still too early to tell if this global market is really taking place. There have been some success stories. A few writers are jump-starting careers this way, but it's going to be an uphill climb for awhile. "We're coming in and finding the quality material, and if we can develop that [positive] reputation, we'll be fine," says Brent Armitage.

"I just spoke to one writer who sent out approximately 250 query letters," says Script Shark's Kashiba. "He received responses from forty. Of those, thirty-five were the standard issue, 'We do not accept unsolicited submissions,' letters from the company's legal department. Five companies that had no production credits requested the script."

You're doing well with your snailmail query letters if you can get above 5% of the companies and agencies you contact to request your script. According to Ed Kashiba, "About 3–5% of our submissions receive either a 'Consider' or 'Recommend' coverage analysis." Other sites have reported similar numbers. In most cases, you need your script to receive a high mark before it will be passed on to producers or agents, so your chances of success submitting to a script site, compared to letter queries, are about the same.

It's not just a matter of winning over screenwriters, but the industry as well. And it's an industry that I think is slowly coming around. The Web is a logical area of expansion for the industry and the literary marketplace.[7]

My main concern is that these sites are doing nothing more than creating another "slush pile," which is exactly what Hollywood wants to avoid. But the saving grace is that the industry is always in search of new material and talent, and if they can do it cheaply, they will. It's more efficient than phone calls and meetings to log on to a Web site, do a search in a high-powered database, and find coverage for the genre and/or type of material one is seeking.

---

[7]Terry Boorst and Deborah Todd. "Cyber Internetworking: A New Generation of Literary Representatives Surf the Web for 10 Percent." *Written By*, Nov. 2000. Web: *www.wga.org/WrittenBy/1100/alt.html*

Instead of having a stable of readers, companies can utilize script sites for coverage. If the coverage is professional, it makes that much more sense. I'm not saying that production companies will do away with readers. Script sites simply offer them another source.

The biggest complaint you will hear from some industry professionals is the lack of filtering that can be done with some online areas where any-one can access a Web site and post a script, log line, or synopsis. This is how the slush pile is created. When an agent or agency submits a script to a company, chances are it's pretty good or it never would have made it that far in the first place. Studios and production companies have a relationship with certain agents, and they trust them to provide good material.

Good agents and big agencies sell material because they have established these relationships with members of the Hollywood community. This aspect of the business is something that script sites must work on to become important players. Only time will tell if they can.

CHAPTER EIGHT

SCRIPT CONSULTANTS

"The hardest thing about writing is actually knowing what you're going to write."

— Syd Field

Before you even consider hiring a script consultant, keep in mind that they can't write your screenplay for you. As a matter of fact, in most cases, you can't even hire one unless you've got a finished product. And frankly, any consultant who would take money from a writer who has never completed a screenplay is an unethical person. Typically, script consultants are only for screenwriters who have done quite a bit of writing already and need that experienced, critical eye to help them turn their best screenplay into a winner.

With script sites and consultants coming online in growing numbers, the lack of regulation on the Web truly does complicate matters for writers in seek of reliable help. Requiring these services to have licenses or proven credentials would be an improvement. There are services online that are nothing more than scams, consultants who have virtually no credentials or experience, out-of-work readers looking to make a quick two or three hundred dollars, and washed-up professionals seeking to sustain a living by stealing from the dreams of aspiring screenwriters.

Some online script consultants have hit hard times. With the advent and proliferation of script sites, the ones left out in the cold are the consultants. "Although [the] biz is respectable, [it's] slowed enough to concern me," one consultant confessed. With so many more options than just a couple of years ago, the market has been seriously diluted.

Not only is there stiff competition, there is also an underlying belief among a growing number of online screenwriters that some script consultants are only taking advantage of them. "I sent in a couple hundred dollars and my script. What I got back was a log line, synopsis, and a page of notes telling me what I already knew," explained one unsatisfied writer. Finding the right consultant who really cares about helping newbie writers is very important. When a consultant really doesn't care, it shows.

It also comes down to companies with large budgets vs. individual consultants with limited budgets. "They have plenty of money to spend on advertising," adds another consultant. "I mean, they're in every magazine and on every Web site." More and more writers are spending their limited financial resources on submission fees at script sites, not on a consultant.

What is perhaps the biggest disadvantage most consultants face is that they do not, or cannot, offer the same services as the big script sites. When you submit your script to one of those sites, you not only get coverage, but in most cases you get to list your script in a database where producers and agents can find it. And, if your script is exceptional, the script site will often help you get representation or even set up meetings with potential buyers. Most consultants do not help writers shop their screenplays. Some do have connections and will try to help you, but most simply do not have the time or resources. All they can really do is offer advice on how to go about marketing your screenplay.

What most script sites and consultants offer is coverage. It's important to keep in mind that script coverage can be a pretty useless thing, especially if not well done. A lot of what coverage consists of is information you already should know. In some cases all you're getting is a rehash of your story along with a log line and maybe some notes. Paying hundreds of dollars for something you can do yourself just doesn't make a lot of sense. Script consultants are going to have to adjust their services to better fit the ever-changing and expanding Internet market and its users; some already have.

WHAT A GOOD SCRIPT CONSULTANT DOES

A good consultant gives you more than script coverage. You will usually get a thorough breakdown of your script, page by page and sometimes line by line. Every consultant seems to have a different term to describe what it is they do, and, indeed, some do offer very difference services. But whether it is called a critique, review, evaluation, analysis, or simply notes, they all do essentially the same thing, so don't get confused by the terminology. The main thing is to make sure you are getting more than a log line and a summary of your story. Ask them very specific questions if you're unsure. Ask them for references and success stories — writers who have gone on to sell or option their work.

What consultants really do well is communicate. This is what truly separates them from the script sites. They clearly define what the problems are with the story and how to go about fixing it. They offer examples and notes. They can help you problem-solve by lending a guiding hand. Perhaps most important, with the reputable and well-respected consultants, you'll get to speak with them over the phone. You get to ask them questions. Sometimes you do have to pay extra for it, but I always suggest that you try to negotiate. (Ask the consultant to include the phone call in the fee.) After all, you'll be calling them, so it'll be your dime. Script sites do not offer you the chance to speak with the person who read your screenplay — there are some that don't even list phone numbers.

In rare circumstances, there are some consultants who take exceptional clients under their wing. If you've got talent and you're lucky enough, you can even forge a "mentor" relationship with those few consultants who are willing. Years ago, I was able to find such a mentor, and it was an invaluable experience.

Finally, a good consultant will provide some guidance on marketing your screenplay as well. There are even a few who will connect writers with producers and agents, much as the script sites do. What it all comes down to is a more personal experience and usually a more rewarding one.

THE LISTINGS

In this section, I limited my listings to only those services that have Web sites. There are some very excellent consultants who are not online and hence were left off. I also did not cover every site I found. I wanted to give you a sense of the wide range of different services you will find online. I did not grade or review these services, but simply attempted to cover what they do and what my thoughts about them are. They are not listed in any particular order. I did not submit any material to these sites for review while writing this chapter, though I have had experience with script consultants in the past.

Scriptique — *scriptique.com*
Right away I noticed the site does not list any testimonials or current clients whom you can contact. Inexplicably, I could not find any information on who reads your script and what their credentials are. Their Mission Statement page offered the following: "At Scriptique, we assert that editing and revision are essential components of the writing process." They claim to offer high-quality editing at affordable rates.

According to the site, "At Scriptique, we appreciate the time and effort your screenplay represents, and pledge to honor it by minimizing your frustration through a professional evaluation." The site looks extremely professional, but without any information on it about who they are, it will most likely fail to get many rational screenwriters to send them their scripts and a check. I did contact them requesting credentials, which I do not always do, as this information should be clearly outlined on the site. I got this fleeting response: "Kirk, reader, teacher. BA, Oberlin College. MA English, UC Irvine." I could not find any other information about Kirk.

All of the information on the site is severely lacking in detail.

Costs and Benefits:

Line-by-line Editing Service ($99) — This will get you the following: "Lexical and syntactical suggestions, grammatical, and typographical corrections, and format revisions." All of their fancy talk is a little over-the-top and is not very effective in truly describing what it is they do.

Studio-style Coverage Service ($149) — This is essentially script coverage: log line, story summary and notes. They described this service as providing a very general evaluation, a big-picture approach, according to them.

Comprehensive Critique Service ($249) — This is a "professional evaluation" of every aspect of your screenplay, line by line. No idea on a page range for what you'll get back. The description of this service is fairly adequate.

Scriptzone — *scriptzone.com*
Professional screenwriter Paul Young is a former Columbia Pictures story analyst and is the author of *The Lennon Factor* and *The Nature of Information*. His Web site contains quotes from names you'll recognize, praising his work and writing. Young is not only a consultant, but he also does work for studios and production companies as a "script doctor." Many consider his script notes to be some of the best around.

According to his site, the script analysis you'll receive is "constructive, exhaustive, and uncompromising." A very impressive Web site presentation.

Costs and Benefits:

Screenplay Analysis ($500) — An intensive fifteen- to twenty-page analysis covering all aspects of your screenplay: story, structure, character, dialogue, and then his evaluation and suggestions for improvement.

Additional services:

Book-to-screenplay Analysis ($4.00/ms. page) — This is a nice service, as not everyone offers it. You get a fifteen- to twenty-page analysis of your book manuscript, its strengths and weaknesses, and a determination of its value as a potential motion picture source. He also offers his suggestions on how to best adapt the material.

Script Notes ($350) — Perhaps the best deal for the money. You get an eight- to ten-page analysis of the strengths and weaknesses of your screenplay, along with suggestions on how to fix the problems. Young also gives you some direction for future revisions.

Script Conference ($200) — A one-hour phone or in-person discussion about your script. Essentially "script notes" over the phone, nothing in writing.

Story/Development Conference ($100.00 per hour) — Continual (if you wish) discussions about your material and story ideas. Mr. Young will listen and offer suggestions and feedback during the process.

Hollywood Script Coverage — *www.hollywoodscriptcover.com*
The short descriptions for services they provide, combined with a lack of success stories or endorsements, leads me to be very leery of this one. I also could not find any information on who provides your script coverage and what, if any, credentials they have.

They do claim to have professional readers who will read your script and provide studio-style analysis of your screenplay's strengths and weaknesses, and they will also provide feedback on how to correct any problems.

Costs and Benefits:

Studio-style Analysis ($180) — They focus on the strengths and weaknesses of your story in an attempt to improve salability of your screenplay. (More than ninety pages, add $2 per page.)

Screenplay Services — *screenplayservices.com*
Jon Blosdale has worked as an associate producer for Robert Conrad's production company, where he produced MOWs and television shows. As an independent producer, he has also worked as a script and production consultant for Charlie Matthau's production company and others.

The site is well presented and offers testimonials and e-mail addresses to contact them — a big plus! Clearly Mr. Blosdale has enough experience to provide most screenwriters with some useful information.

His service provides script analysis aimed at not only improving your story, but doing so with an eye to how it will translate when reviewed by a professional studio reader. On the site Blosdale says, "This will help you understand where your script works, and where it needs work, before you begin trying to pitch and market it." I found his short presentation to be informative and interesting. It's one of the more unique approaches that I encountered.

Costs and Benefits:

Coverage Analysis ($295) — From the site: "Avoid your screenplay merely being skimmed by studio executives because the first ten pages didn't do what they were supposed to do." This service provides an evaluation focusing on your script's structure, action, characters, and story. This very specific analysis will help you get your script ready to be covered. No screenplays over 120 pages will be accepted.

Script and Story Consultation ($100 per day) — Daily discussion and consultation in person or over the phone.

He also offers several other services aimed at the studio and production company level.

Screenplay Solutions — *screenplaysolutions.com*
Robert Stetzel has been a member of the WGA since 1976. His credits include such films as *Brainstorm* and *Distant Thunder*. He was the screenwriter of these movies, not a "consultant" or something else. He is a working writer with a recent credit for the 1999 production of *Icarus*. I really like the fact that he's not some washed-up writer living off aspiring screenwriters. So what gives?

"I've been a writer for many years, and I got to a point in my career where I want to give back what I've learned," says Stetzel. "I'd probably do this work for free, but I find that a fee forces a commitment on the writer's part, which keeps them focused. I've actually found the experience enjoyable and satisfying. I've worked with writers from Australia to Ireland. Some of the work is absolutely dreadful, while some is quite good."

177

When you look at the different script consultants, they are all essentially offering the same thing. But what it all comes down to is working with people who really know what they're doing. It's pretty obvious that Mr. Stetzel is one of those consultants. "My approach is to take away the confusion by finding the clear, concise questions you need to ask of your work to empower it forward," explained Stetzel.

The difference between a successful experience and a bad one is obviously the quality. Your odds of having a good experience increase significantly if the consultant you hire has experience.

Stetzel provides writers with an in-depth critique of their scripts.

Costs and Benefits:

Script Critique Notes ($600) — This includes an analysis of your characters, dialogue, and overall structure. He will also offer notes on how to improve these areas. He stresses that these notes will not be abstract. "They are power tools to fix your material — geared not only to make your story more effective, but also the dictates of the current market in order to enhance a sale," says Stetzel.

Mr. Stetzel's presentation on his site is very impressive. My correspondences with him only solidified that feeling for me.

Hollywood Script — *hollywoodscript.com*
Craig Kellem is also a member of the WGA. He is himself a screenwriter and has optioned two screenplays. He mainly comes from a TV background where he has worked as a producer and executive at places such as Universal. He developed and sold the hit series *Charles in Charge* among many others. He started his show business career in New York City as a TV talent agent.

According to the site, there are some very specific reasons why consulting with a script consultant is smart: They can provide a fresh perspective, and, as in Mr. Kellem's case, they have knowledge of the marketplace. And perhaps most important, it's their job to pay attention to the details. Another solid Web site presentation.

Costs and Benefits:

Script Consultation and Script Notes ($175) — Craig first addresses the bigger issues, or what he calls the "macro issues." These include your story, character development, subplots, and theme, which is pretty much the usual fare. However, this is followed up with script notes.

From the site: "I work scene by scene; line by line. I cover everything, the works! And I make specific suggestions on how to fix and improve things." Craig prides himself on a practical and solid consultation. On top of that, you get a phone conference with him, and he even offers to give you his thoughts on tape as well.

If you look at Craig's credentials and experience and combine that with the cost, he's hard to beat. Hollywood Script is a great option for the price.

Scriptmaven — *scriptmaven.com*
Herschel Weingrod has worked in the industry for over twenty-five years as a writer and producer. His credits are very impressive and include *Trading Places, Twins, Kindergarten Cop, Space Jam*, and others. He also produced *Falling Down* and has produced independent feature films and three award-winning short films.

If you have a comedy script, you have to give Mr. Weingrod some serious thought.

Costs and Benefits:

Initial Script Review ($500) — This gets you a critique of your screenplay, which consists of what he calls a "subjective evaluation" of the following elements: plotting, narrative, dramatic structure, characterizations, dialogue, originality, and marketability. (Add $5 for every page over 120.)

Script Rewrite Review ($250) — He evaluates your rewrite and offers feedback and suggestions.

He also offers a phone consultation, which is negotiable. I suggest asking for this to be included in the fees, which are hefty to begin with.

Script Services — *scriptservices.com*

Chris Caldwell claims to be a professional script reader with over six years of experience. "I currently read scripts on a freelance basis for a major studio and a major talent agency and continue to see the same problems as I did when I worked at a boutique agency," says Caldwell on his site. "I have also written a few scripts, so I understand the writing process. The scripts I have written have done fairly well in the entertainment community." If what Chris says on his "Background and Testimonial" page is true, he has had several successful clients, which is important. Good consultants should have several success stories that they proudly share.

I like that he offers testimonials and is an experienced screenwriter himself. Caldwell offers a full range of services covering treatments, outlines, teleplays, and screenplays. He also offers his services as a consultant. "My service is designed for people who truly want to improve their screenplay," adds Caldwell. "The fact is, I enjoy reading scripts and giving notes. For me there is nothing more gratifying than to receive an e-mail from someone whose script I gave notes on, who just sold it or got an agent."

Costs and Benefits:

Treatments and Outlines ($50)
Thirty-Minute Television Script ($60)
Sixty-Minute Television Script ($85)

With the above services you get a log line, summary, and a couple of recommendations and suggestions. The price is right, I'm just not sold on the usefulness of these services.

Script Coverage ($100) — The saving grace here is that it's only a hundred dollars, and he does provide some analysis.

Consultant Services ($200) — This is really the service that Mr. Caldwell wants you to sign up for. "Consultant Services provide you with more valuable details, than that from the basic Script Coverage," says Caldwell. "I demonstrate the strong points of the story and give suggestions for the weaker points. With the consultant services you are also able to e-mail me with questions regarding my comments and I will go over ideas and suggestions for rewrites. Many clients have found this particularly helpful when incorporating my notes."

He also offers a *Consulting and Editing Service* for $350 that appears to be even a little more in-depth and also includes grammar and syntax editing.

Story and Script Development — *storyandscriptdevelopment.com*
If you pay attention to who wins which competition, you'll recognize the name Sandy Eiges; she won the 1998 KASA Screenwriting Award. Not only that, she is now a working screenwriter with several projects in development, including one at Henry Winkler's Fair Dinkum Productions. She also does consultant work for studios and production companies.

According to the Web site, several "writing clients have gone on to sell or option their work." I really like the site's design, and the presentation of her experience and services is very straightforward. No real complaints as far as those elements are concerned. The site also provides testimonials and client feedback.

One important difference I noticed in the services she provides is this: "If and when your project is ready for the marketplace," says Sandy on her site, "I will use my extensive list of Hollywood contacts — agents, managers, development and studio executives and producers — to help you sell your screenplay to Hollywood." That could be worth the lofty fees she asks. Not all consultants offer this service, so this is a major plus.

Costs and Benefits:

Script Evaluation ($750) — Her description of this service is very thorough. She will analyze your story and characters and identify any problems that exist, along with possible solutions. This analysis must be significant as she guarantees ten to twenty pages of notes. (At the time of this writing, she was offering a "special" for $375. I suspect the price will eventually be somewhere between the two.)

General Script Notes ($300) — This is only an option after you have completed a script evaluation with her. These notes consist of a five- to seven-page analysis of your rewrite, which is completed based on her recommendations from the evaluation. I thought this was a nice option but found the price to be a major turnoff.

It looks like you could easily spend over a thousand dollars with her after the initial evaluation and subsequent rewrites. It's hard to justify that much money for any kind of script consulting. It all comes down to her experience and the quality of her evaluation.

Dave Trottier — *davetrottier.com*

I've known Dave Trottier for several years. He's written for me and does so for newsletters and publications. He is also author of *The Screenwriter's Bible*, one of the better screenwriting books on the market. Mr. Trottier has had a Web presence for several years and has helped a lot of screenwriters. Of all the script consultants out there, he's been the most recognizable figure online. There are many who have followed his lead.

Dozens of his clients have sold their screenplays. He has a nice section that offers testimonials and quotes from some of them. Dave is not simply a script consultant, he is also an accomplished screenwriter, having sold several screenplays. He has done quite a bit of work as a consultant for studios and production companies as well.

"As a script consultant, I see myself as an objective third party who reads a client's script and provides a thorough analysis of its strengths and weaknesses," explains Dave. "One word of caution: Don't expect a script consultant to convert your script into a blockbuster. Script consultants provide evaluations and analyses; they seldom do any rewriting nor do they market your script for you." I think that's sound, honest advice coming from one of the most trusted script consultants on the Web. However, Dave is missing an important issue that other consultants have as well: the need to be able to connect exceptional writers with the industry through their proven connections. After all, consultants who have been in business long enough, working as a consultant for producers and production companies, surely have numerous contacts.

Costs and Benefits:

Two-step Evaluation ($475) — A thorough, well-written critique of your script, consisting of eight to fourteen pages of notes. This evaluation is followed up with a telephone story conference. The client can read the evaluation and then ask follow-up questions about the evaluation, including Dave's notes about the story and characters.

Additional services:

Evaluation of three-page story synopsis ($145)
Evaluation of one-page query letter ($85)
One-on-one consultation ($250/hour)

I think that overall you get your money's worth, and I like the "two-step" approach that includes a telephone conversation. There are several services where you will never even speak to the consultant, and if you do it will cost you extra.

Syd Field — *sydfield.com*

There isn't a more recognizable name in the field of screenwriting than that of Syd Field. His books, including *Screenplay, The Screenwriter's Workbook, Selling A Screenplay, Four Screenplays*, and *The Screenwriter's Problem Solver*, are known around the world. On top of that, his consulting services are in high demand. He has served as creative consultant to the governments of Argentina, Austria, Brazil, and Mexico.

Syd Field has collaborated with many of the top writers, directors, and producers in the business, including Roland Joffe (*The Killing Fields*), James Brooks (*Terms of Endearment, Broadcast News*), Joe Esterhas (*Basic Instinct*), and others.

For the past twenty-five years, he has taught and guided thousands of screenwriters and hundreds of professionals. As for his online presence, Syd admits it's kind of a new gig for him. "I'm in a real kind of absorbing situation right now because I feel it's [the Internet] a new educational format you can use to offer online content. I know in my case it's very easy to create courses online because people need to write, and you need to evaluate what they've written. So how to do it?," asks Syd. "That's the real question. You know, it's not like just doing a seven-week class in a school or something. So that's what I'm exploring right now. I certainly want to contribute to expanding the screenwriter's craft [online]."

If you are extremely serious about becoming a screenwriter, you should consider Syd's evaluations, classes, and/or seminars.

Costs and Benefits:

Screenplay Evaluation ($2,500) — A page-by-page analysis of your screenplay with suggestions on improvement. There are several points Syd will cover: making sure you have set up the action and characters effectively, your transitions, character relationships, and your beginning and ending — do they work effectively? After the evaluation is completed, you will also get a personal interview (if you live in the Los Angeles area) or a phone conversation covering the specific points of his analysis. The chance to meet one-on-one with Syd Field is pretty cool. Hopefully you are able to take advantage of it.

Why should you pay so much for Syd Field's services? According to Syd, there's a simple reason. "I think there are so many people writing screenplays that even now the readers don't know how to read screenplays accurately." True experts like Syd and others are almost a slam-dunk when it comes to quality. But when the cost of the evaluation is going to run into the thousands of dollars, I can't recommend that to everyone.

So here's the rub as far as I am concerned: Imagine you are on the verge of writing a great screenplay, but you just can't seem to put it together. Could it be worth the price to have someone like Syd help you? It could mean the difference between having a hobby and a career, so absolutely; or it could mean you'll be borrowing rent money come next month. It's a tough call.

"I hear story development people looking for screenplays at major production companies, bemoaning the fact that there is just nothing out there," adds Field. "The people writing are just not writing good material, or what they're writing has already been done before." This would make script consultants that much more important.

But keep in mind, instead you could buy all of Syd's books for less than $100 — not a bad option.

CHAPTER NINE

MARKETING YOUR SCREENPLAY

When asked by a fledgling filmmaker the best way to break into the moviemaking business, *Star Wars* writer/director George Lucas replied, "Somehow," or at least that's how the story goes. I'd like to think that Mr. Lucas wasn't being sarcastic, and that he really could not offer specific advice. I'm almost positive this story happened before the advent of the Internet, as I'm certain that if presented with the same question today, he would reply with, "The Internet."

Everything is for sale online, from porn to banana-peel artwork. If it can be sold, there is usually a Web site involved. The Internet has spawned a global marketplace for more than just screenwriters interested in selling scripts. You don't need a million-dollar budget to sell your screenplay or movie online. But you will need a plan.

The Web is the ultimate device for direct marketing; you can communicate directly with the consumer and, in your case, the buyer. There are several strategies you can use to market yourself and your screenplay(s). Marketing your script doesn't end with the written word; you're going to have to market yourself simultaneously.

FOUR QUESTIONS TO ANSWER

During the countless hours I've spent online researching and writing this book, I have encountered a lot of aspiring screenwriters. From message boards and FAQ boards, to chat rooms and newsgroups, I've had conversations with hundreds of writers. During this time, I have noticed some questions that seem to come up more than any others:

1. What's the best way to protect my screenplay, WGA registration or a copyright?
2. Do I need an agent to contact most producers?

3. What's the best way to go about contacting an agent or producer?
4. How do I market my script at such a distance from Hollywood?

With answers to these questions, you will be able to develop a course of action to sell your screenplay(s) online. Good luck!

1. A COPYRIGHT IS BEST

Copyrighting your screenplay with the Library of Congress is the best option. It essentially protects your work forever. A copyright lasts for your lifetime plus seventy years, so for all practical purposes, we'll just say forever. To copyright your material, you must download the form from their Web site, print it, fill it out, and mail it along with a copy of your material and $30 to their office. Your copyright is official as of the date it is processed. (Note: you will need an Adobe Acrobat Reader to view and print the form. Most computers come with it installed. If yours does not, find your way to *adobe.com* and download the free program.)

Library of Congress
Copyright Office
101 Independence Avenue, S.E.
Washington, D.C. 20559-6000
(202) 707-3000
www.loc.gov/copyright/

The WGA, on the other hand, will acknowledge your authorship on the date your work arrives, provided of course you have included all the proper materials and fee. A WGA registration is a good way to establish a very specific date of ownership, but it is limited in duration, as it is only valid for five years. The cost is $20 ($10 for members), which must be sent with an unbound copy of your material.

WGA — West
7000 West Third Street
Los Angeles, CA 90048
(323) 782-4500
www.wga.org

Finally, there is another option that is similar to a WGA registration but lasts longer and can be done online, which is a big plus. Not only that, they charge only $18.95 per registration, which lasts ten years.

ProtectRite
(National Creative Registry)
1106 Second Street
Encinitas, CA 92024
(800) 368-9748
www.protectright.com

2. NO, YOU DO NOT NEED AN AGENT

If you have read this book from start to finish, you already know the answer. (In case you're not sure what I mean, revisit Chapters Four and Five.) Nonetheless, let me make it clear once again: There is nothing like having a great agent who can open doors for you. Unfortunately, for almost all of you, the reality is you're going to have to bust down those doors yourself. If your goal is a million-dollar spec-script sale and a headline in *Variety*, then you'd better know somebody.

Let's say you're certain you have the next great American screenplay; you just know it. Okay, here's what you do. Go to the WGA Web site (*wga.org*) and download their list of signatory agents. Focus only on the ones living in and around Hollywood who are proven and are open to receiving query letters (there won't be many). You can find out which agent(s) sold which screenplay and for how much by using a database like *hollywoodlitsales.com*. After you've cross-referenced that list with the signatory list, you'll have a few places to contact.

Next you need to start writing your query letter. You then send out your letter and hope you've written a good one because if you can't even write a good query letter, no one is going to believe you can write an entire screenplay.

Now, it's time to cross your fingers and pray that even one or two agents will ask to read your script. If you're lucky they will. Then, it's a lock. If your script is pure genius, they'll sign you in a heartbeat, and you're on your way. But keep something in mind: There have been plenty of million-dollar scripts that were turned down time and again, for whatever reason, by numerous agents and companies until a sale finally happened. Let's hope you don't have to deal with any of that.

3. E-MAIL IS BEST

Chapter Four provides you with information on how to contact producers and agents with e-mail queries. You're going to focus on the smaller agencies and companies, the ones who want to hear from you. They represent your best shot at getting your material read. Just try calling, and when you get stonewalled by that secretary or assistant, or you get voicemail, you'll be scrambling for your computer. After sending out dozens of letter queries without a response, you'll be surfing the Web in no time.

Your goal is to establish yourself. If you're a good writer, you can get an independent producer to read your script, and he or she will in turn recognize your talent and make your movie. Once you have that all-important first credit or sale, you can then query the big agencies.

4. INTERNETWORKING

Everything in this book has been leading up to this chapter. This book is intended to help you sell your script online. There is a global literary market developing. It's getting bigger and better every day. You haven't missed out on it yet — it's just getting started.

The driving force behind this is what is known as internetworking: the direct interaction with agents, producers, and production companies by aspiring writers — something that hasn't always happened. Your goal is to start a career, and internetworking will be the means by which you will succeed. If you're serious about becoming a professional screen-writer you already know that moving very close to Hollywood will most likely be a must someday. But for now, don't worry about that. When the time comes to move, you'll know.

It's really not that complicated. You're going to contact anyone and everyone. You're going to hustle. Those who work at it the hardest will succeed. There isn't a magic formula to selling a script. Hard work, perseverance, and commitment will get you halfway there; a great script will do the rest.

- *Script Sites* (Chapter Seven): You'll want to post your log lines and synopses on as many free sites as possible. Your first stop should be *hollywoodlitsales.com*. Post your material in their database, then check out their "Producers Seeking Material" board where inde-pendent producers and companies post want ads. Next you'll want to target a couple of the pay sites. I recommend Writers Script Network, Script Shark, Storybay and Studio Notes.

- *Enter Contests*: You'd be surprised how winning a contest can gain you instant credibility, especially if it's one of the bigger ones. Entering contests and using script sites all comes down to your financial situation; hopefully you can do a few of each. I highly recommend the Nicholl Fellowship (by the Academy of Motion Picture Arts and Sciences) and Chesterfield. For a complete list of contests, see Chapter Three.

- *Message Boards* (Chapter Two): Find every message board where it is allowed to post information about your script. Be sure to check with the site administrator first, as many sites do not allow this. They call it "spamming," and the punishment can be death by verbal assault.

- *Literary Markets*: Try writing for a screenwriting Web site or a publication. I have over a dozen writers whom I pay periodically for material. But it's not the money they do it for — it's the exposure. Kenna McHugh was contacted by a publisher who saw her writing on the site, and the result was her book *Breaking into Film*. Screenwriter John DeMarco used to do Q & A for my site. He often told me how he established many industry contacts from the board. One turned into a movie deal with an independent producer.[1] As for myself, I met my publisher for this book through my Web site, as well as several producers who offered options for my screenplays. So the point is this: Do not be still, always be active. Getting exposure for yourself can be a great device for acquiring contacts.

- *Create a Home Page*: A personal home page can act like a virtual business card, or it can be much more. You can list your contact information and nothing else. You can add your photo, bio, log lines, synopses, and entire screenplays. There has been some debate in the past about how effective a home page really is in marketing your screenplay, but I think it can go a long way in helping you get noticed. Besides, can you afford not to do it?

GET AN 800 NUMBER

At *efax.com* you can get your own toll-free telephone number, free of charge. On top of that, you can set it up so every message is sent to you by e-mail, or you can have it forwarded to your home phone number. Agents or producers can use this number to contact you immediately to request your material. The fact that it is a free call makes them more likely to use it right away. You can't imagine what the phone bill for an agency or company is every month. Having a toll-free number is also a courtesy, something that will separate you from everyone else. I've had an 800 number for years, and it has been invaluable. Make sure to place this number in your e-mail signature (see Chapter Four) and on your home page.

---

[1] Unfortunately, John passed away before he could complete it. John was the first professional screenwriter to contact me back in 1996 and volunteer his time to answer questions for aspiring screenwriters on my site. I will always be thankful to him for that.

CREATING YOUR HOME PAGE

Here's a crash course on creating your very own home page. First, you need some real estate, a virtual lot on which to build your home. You can obtain a free page on the Screenwriters Utopia Planet,[2] a very easy-to-use program that allows you to post almost anything with absolutely no knowledge of HTML or FTP (file transfer protocol). You pick a user name and a password and then create your page.

There are plenty of other free home-page services as well: *hollywood.net*, *hollywoodnet.com*, *geocities.com*, *tripod.com* and many others. I suggestion staying away from generic free home-page sites like Geocities, and use one that deals with screenwriting or Hollywood in some way. It makes you look more professional.

Second, to make the most effective home page, you'll need to know some basic HTML (hypertext markup language).

To place a space between paragraphs	\<P>paragraph\</P>
To place a line break	\
To bold your text	\<B>bold text\</B>
To italicize your text	\<I>italicized text\</I>
To create a link	\<a href="http://whatever.com">link title\</a>
To add an image	\<img src="link to image">
To link your e-mail on a page	\<a href="mailto:me@aol.com">e-mail\</a>
Pre-formatted text, like your script	\<PRE>your script text here\</PRE>

With these basic HTML commands, you can create your home page and add pretty much anything you would need for prospective producers to contact you. You could even post part of your script online if you wanted.

Third, keep your Web page simple, attractive, and easy to navigate. Do not use a lot of different colors or fonts. Consider it much like something you would hand out at a conference. You want it to look as professional as possible.

---

[2] *www.screenwritersutopia.com/planet/login.htm*

Finally, announce your site to search engines and directories such as *yahoo.com*, *altavista.com*, and *go.com*. But most importantly, give out your Web address to everyone you know. Make sure to include it in your e-mail signature and along with your contact information on screenplay submissions. If you have business cards, make sure to include it and your e-mail address.

POSTING YOUR SCRIPT ONLINE — IS IT A GOOD IDEA?

Ignorance is bliss. This is the only reason I can come up with to explain why someone would post an entire screenplay online for everyone and anyone to read. The logic some have argued is this: There are tens of thousands of screenplays registered and/or copyrighted each year; 99% of these will never be sold or made into a movie, so why would anyone steal one? Then why would they bother reading one? Besides, they won't steal the whole screenplay; they'll just steal your story.

"Posting an entire script online, to me, isn't reasonable unless it's in a highly controlled environment," says professional screenwriter Jenna Gelfand. "For example, the American Zoetrope site — there, the site administrators keep a log of everyone who has ever downloaded a copy of a script. Every visitor must be registered with valid contact information. Just posting your script on any old Web page seems like asking for trouble to me. Besides, I know very, very few industry professionals who will ever want to read a whole script online. A synopsis should be enough. If you've done your job properly with the synopsis, you shouldn't have any trouble getting producers to request hard copies of the script."

Very few producers, readers, or development executives will spend much time visiting personal Web pages on instructions from you. There are a very small percentage that do, and that's why I think you should have a home page, but not for the purpose of posting your entire screenplay.

I'll take this one step farther. Let's say there is a producer who sees your screenplay online and starts to read it. "Man, this is pretty damn good," this producer thinks to himself. He prints it out, all 120 pages. He reads it. Now what's to stop him from taking your idea, finding someone to unknowingly write a script based on it, and making a movie? How are you going to prove he stole it? If this producer is smart, he'll just steal your great concept and develop a similar but different story. This is no more far-fetched than the mentality that leads someone to place their screenplay online to begin with.

Now consider this: You only post a log line and/or synopsis for this script, maybe even the first couple of pages. This producer reads your well-written log line and synopsis, loves the idea, and begrudgingly contacts you requesting the script. He has now started what some attorneys call "the handshake." A paper trail has been established. So now if he tries to steal your story, you have evidence that he contacted you. You would never have this if you posted the entire screenplay online.

My final argument: No one reads online — at least nothing over a few pages. It's too stressful to the eyes and time-consuming to read online. Most people print out something they want to read and save it for a later time. They might print out a four- or five-page document, but not an entire screenplay... that is, of course, unless they are planning on stealing your story.

CHAPTER TEN

THE INTERVIEWS

THE SCREENWRITER'S ADVOCATE: AN INTERVIEW WITH PRODUCER ADAM KLINE

"By the way, what is my Web site address?" producer Adam Kline asked after our interview. Though he may not know what his Web site address is, you'll want to know. "That's how long it's been since I've been on it. I've been extremely busy." This is understandable when you consider what he has been up to the past year.

In early 2000, Adam signed an overall deal with Lion's Gate Films, one of the major independent studios in the business. Lion's Gate has produced some of the top independent films of the last several years, including *The Big Kahuna*, starring Kevin Spacey and Danny DeVito, and recently *Shadow of the Vampire*, an outstanding film. It stars Willem Dafoe and John Malkovich and boasts an excellent screenplay by scribe Stephen Katz.

I first interviewed Adam three years ago, and he hasn't changed. Willing to talk, very open, friendly and, most important, a champion of sorts for the unknown screenwriter, he is making a career out of discovering talent on the Web. Back during our original interview, Adam confessed that he needed the unknown writer "as much as they need me." That's something that aspiring screenwriters forget: There are those people in Hollywood who need you as much as you need them.

Hollywood will always need new material, fresh new talent. I consider Adam one of the early pioneers. He has used the Web to his advantage and at the same time has helped many aspiring screenwriters get their first break. Adam accepts e-mail pitches from his Web site, sometimes getting twenty-five or more per day. After reading this interview, you may want to contact him.

Adam's current project slate includes *Dear Rosie, Johnny Dynamite, Mirror Image*, and several others.

Chris: How do you respond to e-mail queries?

Adam: I request that the writer send a five- to seven-page sentence summary of each feature-length script. If you can write a great summary, then chances are you can write a screenplay.

The reality is that it would be too difficult for me to be involved in teleplays from unknown writers, even though I do a lot of TV. It's just too hard with unknowns. But as far as features or MOWs, it really doesn't make any difference if the writer is an unknown. I work well with the unknown and unrepresented writers.

Also, I really suggest that writers send me summaries for all of their screenplays. You'd be surprised — a writer once sent me fifteen projects, and it was Number Fifteen that he did six years ago that I loved, and I optioned it. So I suggest that writers just get it down and send all of them in one wave.

On your Web site you give writers some guidelines for how to query you. What advice do you have?

I won't download attached files or open them. I don't want attached files at all, or instructions to go to a Web site. Just e-mail me, I don't have that kind of time to go to someone's site. It's that simple. When I do, I usually e-mail them back requesting that they send me their summaries.

Of your current projects, which came from e-mail queries?

The projects I've set up over at Lion's Gate came from the Web site — all of the last five projects, as a matter of fact. They queried me. I liked the ideas enough that I asked to read the scripts, and I optioned them. It happens all the time with me.

Has anything transpired since those developments?

I literally just started my deal [with Lion's Gate] and transferred over the rights to three projects. So now they're at Lion's Gate. The writers are obviously very happy that they're now at a studio. And once a writer is at a studio, he or she has a good chance of getting assignments based on what they've already written.

You can find Adam's site at: *hollywoodnet.com/arkpix/*

AN INTERVIEW WITH FREDERICK LEVY, VICE PRESIDENT OF DEVELOPMENT AT MARTY KATZ PRODUCTIONS

"Everybody has either written a script or knows somebody who has. I truly believe in today's day and age that it's one hundred percent true."
— Frederick Levy

"I went back to my ten-year high school reunion recently and was amazed at how many people knew what I was up to," Frederick Levy told me before our interview. In 1988, Frederick made his way from Massachusetts to California, where he ended up graduating from USC; he majored in business, not film. "I wanted so much to be a part of the moviemaking industry."

During this time he started his career as a studio tour guide at Universal Studios in Hollywood. Having to start a career from such humble beginnings could explain why he would be surprised that anyone would know what he has accomplished. But if you look closely, it's quite obvious.

Not long after, he found himself working as a television guest coordinator for more than a dozen game shows, including *The Love Connection*. This led to a stint as a radio producer for *The Morning Magazine* on KWNK in Los Angeles. Soon he was working for producer Marty Katz, where he distinguished himself as an intelligent and resourceful assistant. Since 1995, he has been involved in such films as *Man of the House*, *Mr. Wrong*, *Titanic*, and *Reindeer Games*.

If that isn't enough, he is also the best-selling author of *Hollywood 101: The Film Industry*, which was his first effort at writing a book.

Frederick's journey is simply remarkable, which made him an obvious choice as an interview subject for this book. He is a leader among his peers in his openness and acceptance of the Internet as a viable source for new material. You contact him at his Web site: *www.hollywood-101.com.*

Chris: Frederick, what do you do to relieve the stress from a high-profile job such as yours?

Frederick: The biggest thing that I do is go to the gym. If I stay in shape, eat healthy, and exercise, I find that I can go so much farther. It's the only "me" time I really get. It's something I do by myself. It's a couple hours per day I can relax, work out, and relax my brain and just chill out. Other than that I tell people, "Yeah, I work a lot, but don't feel sorry for me." I mean, what is my job? I go to fancy lunches every day that some-body else pays for. I get to see lots of movie screenings, read great scripts, meet talented actors, directors, and writers whose work I really admire.

Were you ever intimidated in the beginning? Didn't you start out as an assistant?

I started at the bottom as an assistant, scheduling meetings, getting coffee, picking up the laundry, you know. And yeah, I guess I was probably intimidated at first. This is an industry I knew about and wanted to be a part of. I didn't know where I would end up, and you know, I just wanted to make a good impression. Making a good first impression is what I truly believe helped me make my mark on this company and rise through the ranks. I've been here [Marty Katz Productions] for over six years. I started as an assistant, and today I am vice president of the com-pany. I'm producing films with my boss [Marty Katz].

How was it when you were first starting out? How did the reality compare to say, a movie like *Swimming With Sharks*?

There are some people like executive Buddy Ackerman [the character Kevin Spacey played]. It's funny, I teach a film class, and the first film I show every year is *Swimming With Sharks*. There is some truth to that. Without naming any names, there are some producers in town with similar reputations. It's not everyone, but what you need to understand is that movies cost millions of dollars to make. Every decision is critical because there is so much money on the line. Things need to be done to perfection, and they need to happen on time, so you need to be sharp and on top of things. If somebody says they want Equal and not Sweet 'n' Low... there's a reason. It may seem silly in the movie, but if someone needs something specific, that's what they get. It's a completely different mentality; the work ethic in Hollywood that I have found is not the same anywhere else. For the people working in this business, it's really a lifestyle. It's not a nine-to-five job. It's bigger than you or your career. You have to adapt to that.

How do you utilize the Web in your everyday activities?

I do so much business via e-mail. A lot of my job is being on the phone, tracking scripts, talking to agents, speaking with writers, talking with other producers — and most of that can now be done through e-mail. Instead of calling back and forth a million times per day, I can e-mail. We're doing a movie right now called *Frailty* that Bill Paxton is directing. I can e-mail the director, other producers on the project, and my line producer. It's a really efficient way to communicate and send documents. That's probably the biggest thing. Also, the Web is an incredible resource for writers. Never before did they have such easy access to executives in Hollywood like myself. Through my Web site [*hollywood-101.com*], you can e-mail my company a query letter. We tell you exactly the type of projects we're looking for. If you have something like that, you can e-mail me directly. If I am interested, I'll e-mail back asking for the script. It's that simple.

There are other sites like ours where, if you're computer literate, you can find all sorts of different companies online and get them interested in your screenplays. I also moderate a forum on *creativeplanet.com* called *Hollywood 101: Breaking Into the Business*, where they can network online. They can ask questions, meet other people with similar interests, and give advice. So that's my forum, and *creativeplanet.com* has about a hundred other forums covering various areas of interest, from producing to writing. It's a pretty incredible resource they have.

How many e-mail queries do you get per week?

Between e-mail, regular mail, and fax I probably get about two hundred queries per week. About half of those are e-mail. I have a very large presence online.

Out of those e-mail queries, how many scripts on average do you think you request?

Out of about a hundred query letters, I'll request one, and maybe out of a hundred of those there will be something I'm interested in. So those are tough odds, but they pretty much mirror any other material I get. Just because a project comes through the Internet doesn't mean it's any less desirable than something submitted to me by an agent. I read just as many bad scripts sent in by agents as I do from the Internet. I truly believe great material can come from anywhere.

Off the top of your head, are there any writers who have made it after initially contacting you via e-mail?

Yeah, there's a guy named Gregg McBride who wrote a screenplay called *Vampire Cheerleaders on Spring Break*. I loved the title. I just thought that sounded so funny, I had to read the script, and I loved it. I had him come in for a meeting, and I really thought he was filled with some great ideas. This was about two-and-a-half years ago, and we've tried to do something with the script, but like with any project you have your ups and downs. But anyway, he went on to write a couple other projects. He sold a couple other movies and went on to sign with an agent. I really like to think I hand a hand in helping him. Now he is a staff writer with MTV's *Undressed*. Like I said, he's had a couple of movies made.

Your e-mail address is so accessible. Does the amount of incoming e-mail ever get to be too much?

I have a staff of readers, but I actually look at all of my own e-mail. I have a story editor who deals with all of the fax and query letters, but I read all of my own e-mail. It gets a little overwhelming. Sometimes I have a hundred or so waiting for me. But I love it. I love the feedback. I love hearing from people, both the positive and negative feedback. It makes me feel good when I can help out. You know I also teach. I like to give back. I've been teaching for a few years now at the L.A. branch of Emerson College, UCLA Extension, and the USC Summer Production Workshop.

What do you dislike about e-mail?

Well, here's what I don't like: if I happen to be online working and I get an Instant Message from a colleague. If you're a writer who happens to have me on your IM list, don't send me messages. I am online to work. That's not appropriate. Like I said, I try to be extremely accessible. You can e-mail questions. Just don't start sending me messages.

You're not the norm for larger production companies. Your accessibility is not commonplace among your peers. Do you agree with that?

I'll tell you this: I think that I am at the forefront of a movement that will happen in the future. I've already noticed since I first started looking for material on the Web — I literally started maybe six years ago, that so many more people from some prestigious companies have become more accessible as well. They may not be advertising it as much as I do. I know an awful lot of major companies that do have some sort of a Web presence. Steve Tisch is all over the Web right now, as is Warren Zide. These are pretty big companies. So I was one of the first, but not the only [one].

But Zide and Tisch, if I am not mistaken, are mainly offering a service where writers can send in their script or log line.

Yeah, but even before they were trying to capitalize on it, they were there looking for material as well. And you know what? They still are.

Do you see those Web sites that allow writers to submit scripts — and producers to request them — as a good thing?

Yeah, but you know there are some really good sites that are free to the writer. I think that's how it should be. There's one called *hollywoodlitsales.com*.

It's a very good site; it's free to the writer. That's where I found McBride's script.

About two years ago, Brenden Bernhard wrote an article in *L.A. Weekly* about tracking sites that executives use to discuss projects. Are you familiar with these sites?

Yeah, some of them.

Do you find them handy?

Well, here's the deal: yes and no. When I was starting out, I used them a lot more than I do now. There's a lot of tracking sites, like *ifilmpro.com* for instance, where as an executive you can join and confer with other development people about who's going out with a spec script, because you don't want to miss anything. I did that a lot when I was starting out because I was concentrating a lot of my efforts on tracking projects. Now I have a story editor, and that's his primary focus. So that's not really what I am doing with my daily activities anymore, but somebody in my company is certainly doing that. Absolutely.

Do you use Web sites like *darkhorizons.com* and *aintitcoolnews.com* for daily news?

All of them. The first thing I do is read the *Variety* and *Hollywood Reporter*, the *L.A. Times* Calendar section, *New York Times*; but throughout the day I will visit those sites if I have the time.

Is your use [of the Web news and gossip sites] more for information or for a good laugh?

More for a good laugh.

AN INTERVIEW WITH
SCRIPT SHARK CO-FOUNDER ED KASHIBA

Chris: What do script sites like Script Shark offer writers?

Ed: Well, I won't speak for the others, but Script Shark does two things: One, we provide industry-standard coverage reports that are generated by studio/agency/production company–experienced readers. It's very difficult for a writer to receive a professional, objective analysis of their work. Coverage reports are a fact of life in Hollywood. Nearly every submission to the agencies, studios, and production companies gets a coverage report generated by an industry reader. Two, access. If a Script Shark submission receives a positive coverage analysis, we give that writer and project exposure to our over 20,000 industry subscribers at *ifilm.com*. In fact, we're proud to announce another success story [1/19/01] where our spec-market posting, *Neon Messiah*, was picked up by producer Anne François [*Nine Months*].

There are two important elements to getting in the door. One, you must have talent. Two, you must have access. Unfortunately, many people who only have access and zero talent sometimes make it as well! Hopefully Script Shark can take care of the access part of the equation. Writers should focus on writing, not moving to L.A. and schmoozing.

What's wrong with script sites?

A few of the sites out there charge writers a fee to merely post their script or log line. Some advertise that all of Hollywood is scouring these sites for material. This is not true. The legitimate Hollywood players have way too much material to read, from agencies alone, to be searching for random projects on the Internet. People only look at material that has been referred or screened from a known and reliable source. Our service was established as a filtering device for the industry. We only post material that has made it past our reader staff, readers that our industry clients know and trust. In essence, we're trying to find the few projects that are worth everyone's attention from the pile of unsolicited rejected scripts. If we were merely posting log lines of every script out there, we would not be providing a service to the industry.

What about agents?

Agents are a necessity in the spec-market business. If it wasn't for them, writers would also have to worry about the business side of things, which can get confusing and ugly. Let the businesspeople do their thing so writers can focus on writing.

Can't writers accomplish the same thing with a query letter and without the hefty fees?

Query letters are probably the most over-hyped method of getting in the door. I just spoke to one writer who sent out approximately 250 query letters. He received responses from forty. Of those, thirty-five were the standard issue, "We do not accept unsolicited submissions" letters from the company's legal department. Five companies that had no production credits requested the script. Now, do the math. Is it really cheaper to do the query letter thing? Our submission fee is necessary to stay in business. The money goes to our readers and overhead. We do not make money from our submission fees — not much, at least. Besides, writers are getting something for their money, coverage: not a bunch of boilerplate letters from legal departments.

Is Script Shark making money?

We're not making much money off of the submission fees. The way we do make money is from subscriber fees from industry clients. Also, *ifilm.com*, the consumer portal, acquired us in February 2000. *ifilmpro.com*, a subscriber base of Hollywood professionals, is where we get our industry clients. *Ifilm.com* also now owns the *Hollywood Creative Directory*, Film Finders, TV Tracker, Lone Eagle Publishing, etc.

When a script is "Recommended," does that mean that only Script Shark gets to see it?

No. A "Recommend" means the material goes to the *ifilmpro.com* subscribers, not just the Script Shark team. We only post good coverage.

Only a couple of success stories can be found on your site.

As I said, I'd say we're doing okay; we've had several. It's not a matter of the right people seeing the projects posted on Spec Market. Our writers who are posted on Spec Market are being contacted by our industry clients on a daily basis. It's a matter of whether or not the projects interest our industry clients after they've read the entire script. Many of our writers have signed with either an agent or manager, and it will be up to them on how and when they will spec out their work. Many of our writers are rewriting their script for their agents so they can spec it out within the next couple of months. Of course, I always wish we could get more success stories. That's the whole point. Just to give you an idea, I'd say only about 3–5% of our submissions receive either a "Consider" or "Recommend" coverage analysis. So with over 95% of our submissions not even making it onto Spec Market, I'd say we're doing all right.

How many submissions have you had?

Ifilm does not release those numbers.

You said that query letters are a waste of time. Can you explain that more?

There are agents and production companies who are desperate for clients and material, but there's a pecking order with scripts. Agencies send them out in order of importance. They have established relationships with companies. As for the production companies, I mean, I felt guilty as a development exec. I would see all these query letters and know that they had no chance.

We're giving writers the chance to get read by an industry-experienced reader, and they get to see their coverage. Not every A-list writer gets that. And it's a requirement for us that they are a working reader — no unpaid interns like some of the production companies use. I would know; I used to be one of those interns.

It's all professional, organized, and we have a stable of readers — over twenty.

But are you concerned that one of your "working readers" will take a script to their bosses, but not to you?

We take every precaution necessary. They sign a contract.

Can writers contact and speak with the reader once they have "covered" the script?

No, our readers are not allowed to start a development relationship with submittals. The main reason is because when Script Shark was founded by my partner and myself, it was intended as merely another avenue for us to find product for our companies as well as for our network of friends at the other production companies, studios, and agencies. It was not intended to be a "writer's workshop." We'll leave that up to the various screenwriting schools and books.

So instead you've started doing story notes?

Yes, we have since started a story notes service that provides studio-style development notes that are more comprehensive and helpful in developing a script [than coverage], but we did that with hesitation as well. It was basically because a few of our readers, who are or used to be development executives doing notes all of the time, really wanted to try and help out these writers.

What is the significance of script coverage?

The coverage reports we generate *are* just a by-product in our search mechanism for new talent and projects. By sending the coverage back to the writer, we do two things: One, we give writers not "in the know" a shot of reality on what really happens to scripts submitted in Hollywood. Two, they get a peek at what is typically an internal document at the production companies, agencies, and studios. Even A-listers can rarely get their hands on coverage of their scripts. Giving people a look at what the typical industry reader might write up on their script is an invaluable service — no sugarcoating by their agent.

The WGA doesn't look kindly towards script sites. Is it fair?

They're not against us! We are not a management company. There are those who charge just to send scripts in; the WGA does not look kindly on *those*. We're charging for coverage. Other companies sometimes attach themselves in some producer capacity to the project. We don't, so that's a major difference.

THE BIG DEAL:
AN INTERVIEW WITH THOM TAYLOR

Before he authored *The Big Deal: Hollywood's Million-Dollar Spec Script Market*, Thom wrote for various publications including *Variety*, *Locations*, and *Movieline*. Not only that, he has worked in the industry for such filmmakers as Oliver Stone, Tim Burton, and Ed Feldman.

Chris: You've worked in the industry for some big names, written for several publications, and of course you have a book (*The Big Deal*). What have you enjoyed doing most?

Thom: Each job has its different pluses and minuses, but I would say the work I did with *Variety* magazine was very interesting. I did location scouting for a lot of films, which was interesting. I also really liked agency work too. We represented many writers and helped them get their first major deal, which was really exciting.

Your book, *The Big Deal*, is a great study of the spec market. What was your motivation behind writing it?

I was reading for Oliver Stone and would see these scripts that sold for a million-plus. I would read them and see that they were no different in terms of quality than so many others that did not sell. I wanted to make the book an in-depth study of the spec-script sale process, so I spent three years doing research and interviews.

Also, I had seen a lot of books that dealt with how to sell the script, but nobody had a book on how Hollywood buys the script. So in essence, I turned the system on its head. For example, you're the chairman at 20th Century Fox. What are the dynamics in determining what you buy? It was a fascinating approach from my perspective. Writers need to understand what goes into a spec-script sale; they need to know the process, the ups and downs.

As far as the impetus for writing the book, that was Patrick Sheane Duncan. He is a friend of mine, and after he made $2.5 million for *Courage Under Fire*, I sat down and interviewed him. Afterward he told me he was starting a magazine and wanted me to write an article. That was the basis for the book.

The book's theme — if you got it, and I think a lot of the critics did — dealt with the vision of what a spec script embodies. The successful films understand the vision of the writer, and followed through with that. I think all these books on writing are good in their own way, but you can't instruct someone on how to write, you really can't. And you couldn't write a book and instruct somebody on how to be a great musician. It all comes down to talent.

The main thing for writers is to understand the process. When trying to break in, everyone wants an agent, but with *While You Were Sleeping* [written by Fredric Lebow and Daniel Sullivan], a producer was the catalyst. You don't have to have an agent to sell.

After the failure of the pitch boom of the early '80s, the 1988 WGA Strike is considered to be the origin of the great spec boom. Were there any other significant factors?

The spec boom really started in 1990. There were specs that sold before, of course. Up until the mid-eighties, the thrust of writing a script was more a calling card. They weren't the high concept that they came to be in the late eighties and early nineties. Writing on spec was a way to get into the business, get meetings, and get hired essentially. The studios would have the projects they wanted to do, and they would simply hire a writer to do it. Executives were seen more as creative directors than they are today, though you could certainly argue that some executives today are much like their predecessors.

Script tracking developed as a result of the spec boom. How important are trackers in today's spec market?

I think it's changed. When the spec market was the driving force in the industry, the trackers gained a lot of notice. You could be a valuable tracker and not know much about writing or filmmaking. Now the real important people in town are the ones who can put the elements together, the packaging element. The buyer needs to be able to get the film done. It's geared more toward the individual with the vision to put the movie together. They are the driving force behind the project.

Are the new script sites and tracking sites going to change that anytime soon?

No, I really don't think so. I personally have a problem with most of them, and in a lot of ways I think they just take advantage of screenwriters.

Do you see the global market that the Internet is creating as a tool that writers should use aggressively? There are a growing number of production companies and producers with a presence online.

Not any time soon. Here's the real key: While it's true it levels the playing field, the credibility and genuine nature of the people behind these sites is questionable. That's why something like a *Project Greenlight*, with guys like Ben Affleck, Matt Damon, Chris Moore, and Harvey Weinstein behind it, became so popular. I think that model will continue to do well on the Internet.

Let's not forget that the script is always going to be the catalyst. The Internet does offer writers a lot more opportunity to show their material. The best route for exposure is a credible competition. *Project Greenlight* is an example of that — 8,000 scripts, and only one will get made. So the Internet can be the great equalizer, but not until you've received recognition. When working at an agency, if I got a letter saying that this writer was a finalist in such a competition, then the value of that query letter significantly increased. But even then, there are a lot of other factors involved. I'm not an advocate of sending a hundred blind queries thinking that you're going to get their attention, because you're not, unless you had some success that can separate you from everyone else.

Another problem is that 95% or more of the screenplays submitted to these sites need improvement. Writers need to learn how to help themselves as writers first. In many cases, it can do more harm than good. Script coverage, for example, is essentially what writers should already know about their material. I can't understand why a writer would pay for that.

Everyone in Hollywood is always looking for the great screenplay, but they're going to find it without looking over the Internet. That may change; good material does find a way. It doesn't matter where you're from or who you are; if you have a hot script that has, as they say, "legs," it will walk on its own. That's the main thing you want to develop.

One final note on these sites, and something writers tend to forget: The fewer people who see your spec script, the more valuable it is.

With the possibility of an upcoming strike among WGA, SAG, and DGA members, what do you anticipate happening as a result — another spec boom?

Well, there already were a lot of scripts bought in anticipation of a possible strike, and there were some big sales, but not a lot. Studios are stockpiling some material. The town will close down to a degree, even if there isn't a strike, as they're rushing ahead with so many projects.

The independent market could be a good option, presuming there is a strike. Those who are still in the business will be more open to looking for new writers. That's not to say they will be willing to sign people, just more likely to give you a chance. There will be an increase in work being read.

Would you agree that there are more writers than ever trying to become professionals, yet there are fewer and fewer screenwriters actually writing motion pictures?

That's probably true. People generally tend to follow the money. I'm really curious how many people are bona fide writers of screenplays. Having worked on the agency side, I would request a script based from a good query, and the writing would be just awful. I quickly learned that it was not in my best interest to spend a lot of time with query letters.

I noticed on your site, *bigdealnews.com*, that you offer a script service. Can you tell me a little about that? What do you do?

I do some script critiquing. It's solely from the Web site. It's not something I focus on. I don't really solicit or encourage business. I work with a lot of produced writers mostly, getting their material set up.

I can't guarantee that the script is going to sell, but I can guarantee I will improve the material and offer a better chance of the writer getting that recognition.

When should a writer consider a service like yours?

If a writer feels that creatively they need a fresh perspective of their screenplay, or maybe they need somebody with an idea of what Hollywood looks for, then I think it's a good idea to use a credible script consultant. When one believes their script is as good as it can be, then one of these script sites could be an option.

Is the Web really a visual medium more than a literary one?

The visual medium is at a stage where you want everyone to see it; the literary value correlates to how few people have seen it. You want a script exposed with a strategy in mind.

What you mainly want to do is get a movie made — the visual representation of your work. *The Blair Witch Project* proves that anybody who's serious has the potential to at least do it. With digital filmmaking you can now realistically make your movie.

The exciting thing about the Internet are sites like *ifilm.com*, *atomfilm.com*, and the exposure to all the film material out there. There has not always been a lot of attention paid to short films. Tim Burton built up his career on a couple of short films. The 1990s has led the way in recognizing these short-filmmakers.

In the 1970s and 1980s, the spec script was your calling card; now they like to pop in a tape or go online.

213

AN INTERVIEW WITH SCRIPT CONSULTANT
DAVE TROTTIER

It would take several pages just to cover the amount of experience Dave Trottier has. Let me mention just the highlights. As a script consultant, he has helped his clients sell their material, place in contests, and find writing assignments. His book, *The Screenwriter's Bible*, is fantastic, and I highly recommend it to every aspiring screenwriter.

He has published dozens of articles for publications such as *Script Magazine, Writer's Digest, Hollywood Scriptwriter, Road & Track*, and *USA Today*. But most importantly, he is an accomplished screenwriter, having optioned several screenplays. He has also worked as a consultant helping to develop projects for several major production companies.

Chris: How long have you been involved in screenwriting?

Dave: Nearly twenty years, but I spread my time between teaching, consulting, and writing.

What is your experience as a screenwriter?

I have sold several screenplays and developed projects for The Walt Disney Company, Jim Henson Pictures, York Entertainment, and New Century Pictures. Titles include *Igor's Revenge* (produced); *Zorro, the Gay Blade* (produced, but not credited); *The Comeback Kids*; *Ratman From Saturn*; *Kumquat*; *The New Musketeers*; *Hercules Recycled* (which I also co-produced); and *A Window in Time*. Most recently, my screenplay *Finders Keepers* was produced as *Global Pursuit* and will be released later this year. I am currently co-writing *A Summer With Hemingway's Twin*, an inspiring story about the Hemingway women.

Do you consider yourself a script doctor, script consultant, mentor, all three — what and why?

I am a script consultant, although I have done some mentoring as well as script doctoring for producers and writers. As a script consultant, I see myself as an objective third party who reads a client's script and provides a thorough analysis of its strengths and weaknesses. The written evaluation is followed up with a telephone story conference. That way, my client can read the evaluation and then ask follow-up questions about the evaluation, the story, and the script.

Your book, *The Screenwriter's Bible*, is highly regarded. How did you come up with the idea to write it?

The idea came through my national seminar. I noticed that developing screenwriters across the country had a genuine thirst for knowledge, but seemed confused with the information available at the time. For example, the major formatting book was difficult to read because it was created for professional writers crafting shooting scripts (as opposed to spec scripts). At the same time, writers were being told conflicting things by teachers and other wannabe writers. I could see a tremendous need for a clear and concise explanation of not just formatting, but every aspect of screenwriting, including spec writing and selling. At first I was going to write three different books, but then I decided to put everything under one cover. That way, developing screenwriters could get everything they needed, starting with the fundamentals, in one book. I was delighted to learn that both developing writers and working writers benefited from the book. And Hollywood insiders endorsed it. It is now in its third edition [2000] and has sold nearly 70,000 copies.

Do you offer online classes?

Yes, occasionally.

Some would say you, and others out there, are taking advantage of the aspiring screenwriter. What would you say to that?

Certainly, not everyone in any business is totally reliable. There is a genuine need for objective feedback, and reputable consultants provide it. In twelve years, I have only had two dissatisfied clients; and with one of those, I had to drag it out of him.

When should a writer seek out someone such as yourself for help?

Before seeking a consultant, a writer should ask himself/herself the following:

A. Have I written at least one complete script? Have I have taken it as far as I can take it on my own?

B. Am I a serious writer; in other words, am I seeking a writing career?

C. Have I sought the wisdom of screenwriting books, publications, seminars, and Web sites such as *screenwritersutopia.com?*

D. Have I solicited feedback from other writers, such as in a writers group? If so, have I looked for patterns in the comments I have received? By the way, some writing contests will provide feedback. Feedback from friends and family is almost worthless.

Once a writer has received feedback from free sources, then he or she should consider a script consultant. One word of caution: Don't expect a script consultant to convert your script into a blockbuster. Script consultants provide evaluations and analyses; they seldom do any rewriting, nor do they market your script for you.

What are a couple of success stories your clients have had?

Besides two Nicholl winners and a National Play Award winner, dozens of my clients and students have sold their work or otherwise become working writers. It just so happens that I received two separate e-mails this week from clients who found L.A.-based, WGA-signatory agents to represent their work, and from a third client who is in the finals for the Nicholl. One of my favorite stories is about a woman who wasn't sure she had talent. I evaluated her first screenplay, and then (as so often happens), she didn't sell it, but it became her calling card, her writing sample. On the basis of that script, she got her first development deal and has been writing MOWs now for about ten years.

Any final thoughts?

Writers write. If you have an idea you think will sell or that inspires you, write it out into a screenplay, and don't be afraid to get your work out there where people can respond to it. Writers also learn. Keep in mind that most successful writers worked hard to get where they are. Although it is true that writing is its own reward, be serious enough about your craft that others will take you seriously.

AN INTERVIEW WITH BRENT ARMITAGE
OF *STUDIONOTES.COM*

As the son of writer/producer George Armitage (*Miami Blues, The Last of the Finest*), Brent has produced *Grosse Pointe Blank* and is a professional screenwriter who has optioned several screenplays, including one that was a collaboration with his father. In March of 2001, Brent launched *studionotes.com*.

Chris: How is *studionotes.com* going to be different from other script sites?

Brent: We give development notes instead of script coverage. We're not trying to make a billion dollars here, we're trying to help writers and aspiring filmmakers develop their projects. We're a third access point for contacting the industry, agents and managers being the others. Once we give the writer the feedback, we're not necessarily done. The big thing is the writer can get a consultation by speaking with the person who did their notes.

What does it cost?

Three hundred dollars per screenplay, which includes five pages of development notes, and a two-week turnaround.

Why development notes instead of coverage?

There's really no reason for a writer to get covered; it's not going to help them. 95% receive a non-recommendation — oh, and a log line and synopsis, which is useless if no one is going to read it. Only 5% get any use out of it. Your script has to be recommended to get attention, and the odds of that aren't very good. It's like the difference between a good agent and a bad agent. They're essentially nothing more than bad agents.

Do you attach yourself to the project or take a back-end fee?

No, we're not agents. We don't attach or take a percentage. We're providing a helping hand. It's going to be great for writers. A first-time writer makes, what, $50,000 against $250,000 — if they're lucky — and you're going take 10% ($5,000) from the guy? That's not right.

Who are your readers?

I've got readers all over the country. They are former development executives, not out-of-work script readers. We offer solutions, not coverage that only points out the problems. We give a helping hand, and we will talk to you over the phone.

For an additional fee?

Right, $100 per hour, but it's worth it to talk to that person. It's much more helpful than just getting a few pages of notes. The writer can ask questions about the story, characters, or whatever.

The big problem with script sites is the lack of success stories. How will you address that problem?

You have to have a reputation. The fact is, nobody in Hollywood really wants to read. The producers certainly don't. That's why there is coverage. It's for the benefit of the producer who doesn't want to read, not the writer. We're offering something different, and we're offering more. We're coming in and finding the quality material, and if we can develop that [positive] reputation we'll be fine. The big thing is not attaching ourselves to the screenplays.

Aren't script sites really just creating another slush pile?

With some sites you've got only a 5% chance of someone recommending your script, so what's really the chance of a producer reading your script? We're not just gathering scripts. We'll do, like, only one per week and really do it right.

You're a working writer and producer. Does that make a difference?

Yeah, I hope it does. I really want to help out other writers.

I think it's a big plus. Certainly not everyone in your position would do that.

Some people think I'm pretty silly for doing this.

AN INTERVIEW WITH AUTHOR/PRODUCER
KENNA MCHUGH

Kenna McHugh is a director, producer, writer, and actress who lives and works in California. Kenna has written for my site, and many others, for years and is a well-known and respected online personality. Recently she published *Breaking Into Film*, a how-to guide for anyone interested in starting a career in the film biz.

Chris: Do you use the Internet a lot in terms of advancing your career?

Kenna: I don't rely on the Internet too much. It is still an infant, and the difficulties need to be ironed out, like what caused the dot-com crash. There probably is a formula for Web sites, but not everyone knows it, and many sites are going through growing pains. This can ultimately hurt the writer. I have been stiffed about three times. Writing is hard work, so when I get stiffed it hurts personally and financially.

Wow, that surprises me. From my vantage point, you use the Web a lot. Would you agree that the Internet can help writers?

Yes, I agree; but still, being in Hollywood for the purpose of networking is important. Pamela Gray [*Music of the Heart, A Walk on the Moon*] lives in Northern California but commutes to Hollywood on a regular basis. So does Cynthia Whitcomb [*Buffalo Girls*], who lives in Oregon. I am sure there are more established screenwriters who do commute as well.

This question reminds me of a story about a producer who wrote and directed an independent movie. He needed some guidance — an executive producer — to get the film, *My Sweet Suicide*, distributed. He put his notice on a Web site and found an executive producer. Thus, he got distribution and won awards at film festivals. The executive producer was instrumental in helping him through the process of getting his film in theaters, which wouldn't have happened otherwise. They would never have found each other if there was no Internet.

I primarily use the Internet for obtaining writing gigs. I guess I just don't think it is wise to only count on the Internet as a way to get published or sell a script. Still, you have to be talented and better than the rest.

Tell me about your first "mistake" experience with the Web.

Probably the first mistake I made with the Internet is I didn't take the time to learn all there is about it. I went off of empirical observation and application. I didn't organize my contacts or e-mails properly, so I have lost some really good leads and personal contacts.

With script sites and consultants coming online every day, what advice would you give writers wanting to find some help with their script online?

Be very selective. It's easy for anyone to put up a site and call himself a consultant. Ask for references, and find out if the consultant does workshops. Know before you go — research.

What online services, if any, do you regularly use?

I recommend *hollywoodlitsales.com*. I haven't taken advantage of this site, but should. I know the owner, and he's sharp. Then, I use all the job sites. I check them about three times a week. The posts that interest me, I pitch to.

Writemarket.com is the best site, as the editor sends out a newsletter every Wednesday with less than week-old job postings. She has several e-books that can help fledgling writers.

Also, Coppola has his site, *zoetrope.com*, and Affleck and Damon are working with Miramax on a site [*projectgreenlight.com*] as well that will help screenwriters sell their scripts. There is a downside: You have to work and exchange to get your script noticed.

As a second thought, script consultant Dara Marks put it nicely to me about breaking into film as a screenwriter. "You want to break into that sacred group, and it isn't easy. You have to be better than them; you have to stand out. Once you're in it, great."

Can you tell me a little about how the Web has helped your career? You're a published author.

I met my editor through the Internet and have never met him in person since. We correspond by e-mail and phone. He gave me a writing assignment on a human resources topic for another book. He saw on my e-mail signature — Screenwriters Utopia — and asked if I could write a book about breaking into the film business. I said yes right away. It took a year to get the proposal and contract, but the book deal happened. We got a publisher, advance fee, and acceptance fee. Now, I can promote my book, *Breaking into Film*, at my Web site and other Web sites I write for [Cyber Film School, Utopia] and earn contacts and money.

Also, I have sold lots and lots of articles, not to mention that the Internet is great for research.

Have you established meaningful contacts via the Web? Any interesting stories behind one?

Yes, the founders of Cyber Film School — I wrote some articles for their pilot Web site. Corresponded with Moe Belli, Editor in Chief/Manager. And then, I visited with Moe and CFS publisher Stavros C. Stavrides in Los Angeles. We got to know each other and set a tentative agreement for me to write a monthly column. Today, I am writing for their Web site. I am very proud of this site because it is a virtual classroom for any likely filmmaker or film-career-minded person.

How has your Web site helped you?

My Web site — *www.suite101.com/welcome.cfm/filmmaking* — promotes my book and writing ability and placed me in a role as mentor for quite a few potential moviemakers or film careers.

I have gotten a couple of screenwriting gigs from the site. The gigs were from private parties. One was for writing a master scene list and the other, which I am still working on, is to write a screenplay called *Bite the Hand*.

You've done work in video, television, and film. Is there a Web-related experience that stands out above the others that you can share?

There is a mentoring experience where a young woman benefited greatly by using the Internet to contact me to inquire about breaking into film. She e-mailed me saying she wanted to be a director and asked if I knew how she could get work in film. Ironically, she is now in Hollywood working. She lived in my town. I told her about a book-signing I was doing for *Breaking into Film* and to come on by, and let's talk. She took me up on it, and we talked and exchanged numbers.

Later, I called her up and asked her to help me out with a project I was producing. She did. I observed that she was reliable, hard working, and had a great attitude for the business.

About a year later, I was offered a job to work on a Travolta film. I couldn't because I was committed to another project, but I recommended this young woman. She got the job, worked with Nora Ephron, and launched her career in the film business.

The point is that she took the initiative to surf the Internet, find me, and contact me, and now she's working in the business with a goal to be a director.

AN INTERVIEW WITH MICHAEL GRACE OF SCRIPT STAR PICTURES

Chris: Why try to find screenwriters over the Internet?

Michael: We think that selling a script over the Internet is becoming easier, and it's going to take off. We want to be a part of that. The number of scripts we request from agents compared to the Internet queries, percentage-wise, is about fifty-fifty. So from our perspective, it's a great resource.

As a new company with no credits, how are you going to find funding?

We've already got our funding. We're interested in making a great movie, so we're looking for a great script. We have the money, so we can wait. We do not have a limited window, like most independent companies. If it's twelve months, twenty-four, it doesn't matter. We will wait for the exceptional story and a great script.

As an indie company, what are you looking for in terms of a story?

We don't really consider ourselves to have the business plan of an indie company. We are by definition, but not by mentality. We look at Lion's Gate, and that's what we want to be. As far as what we are looking for, it will change. We will occasionally put out a "call for submissions." Currently, we are looking for a thriller in the $2–5 million range. We're not shooting digital. We're always looking for a very intelligent, character-driven, "actor's movie." We avoid teen exploitative material, and right now we are avoiding high-cost special effects. We're not interested in violence to children or pandering of any type. We'll put out a call for a drama and romantic comedy soon as well.

How have you found the quality of material to be from writers who have contacted you via e-mail?

The quality of material we get is poor sometimes. Some of these kids just don't understand how important it is to have their scripts written well, with proper format and structure. There are a lot of writers who don't actually write screenplays. They don't appear to know the first thing about writing screenplays. Bad grammar, misspelled words, it's incredible sometimes the condition of some scripts that come in. I've even had twenty-two-year-old kids calling, trying to pitch me a movie idea. They think I'm going to pay $100,000 to buy their pitch over the phone.

If it's a great story idea, but poorly executed script, what then?

If it's a very original idea, we will buy the script and have a professional writer do a rewrite. But that would be an extreme case.

You seem to be an advocate for the aspiring screenwriter.

We have great interest in watching screenwriters who we think are talented, but not proven yet. For example, the writers coming out of the big schools like USC and UCLA may not be ready yet. They may need another five years to develop. Writers need to be patient; it takes time to learn the craft.

Do you charge writers a reading fee?

We're not charging writers to send in a script or for us to read it. We do offer an additional analysis service. Writers do not have to take us up on the service to submit. We request scripts all the time, and when we solicit the material, we do not charge, obviously.

With the analysis, we mainly want to help writers improve their craft and become better writers, and it's a great service for only $40. I question it when a company has a contest and charges writers a fee to enter, and that's the way they claim they select material. It's not right. Too many contests are run to make money.

Let's talk about quality of material some more. With an agent you know it's of a certain quality, right?

With agents we know it's going to be in professional format. Some agents work with writers and help them with the script, so the quality is usually better. If they're asking us to pay $1,000 per page, they should have it in the correct format at least. So agents are usually a good filtering device, but we are getting some decent stuff from online submissions.

But most importantly, there is no filter for young writers. They just need to learn what they are doing. For us, if they do spend the money for an analysis, at least we know the material is done correctly.

As far as quality goes, can't a script site filter out the bad material for you?

Let me ask you, who reads for them? For a first-time writer, what kind of analysis do they get back? I think it's a question of whether or not writers will pay for that. I'm skeptical right now. If a writer is going to pay $150, what are they really getting for that? I'm not sure it's the best thing. We'll wait and see. Honestly, I question a lot of these sites that charge for coverage. Why can we do it so much cheaper than they can? I get resumes from other sites' readers, and they haven't been qualified enough to read for us yet.

Do you use readers?

Yes. If I solicit fifty scripts a week, I won't read them all. I couldn't. I'll send some off to a few readers we work with. If they think I should read something, I will.

What's the main goal with your Web site? What do you want to accomplish?

We'll continue developing the site and an online tracking database. We want material to be submitted to us first. We want the first look. That's the name of the game. Speaking of script sites, how does it benefit me to use them? We want to get a hold of the fresh material. That's it. We're not interested in anything that has been shopped everywhere.

Let's say I live in Missouri and I want to submit my script. From my view, there really isn't a site I would use. How do I know a producer or development person will read it if it's good?

Along the same lines of wanting to read scripts first, we're a new company. We're not at the top of the list for the agencies. If they have a hot project, they won't contact us first. We need to go out and find our own material. That's part of why we have this site.

How has your search for fresh talent, new writers, gone so far?

Well, let me say this: We're interested in developing material. There are a lot of passionate writers out here. Hopefully we can find a few and make them successful. It all starts with talent and a great script. I believe we're going to find that perfect script. It just takes a little time.

Do you prefer e-mail queries?

Yes, don't call or send us unsolicited scripts. We won't read them. They won't even be opened.

What complaints do you have about some writers who e-mail you a query?

- Sometimes writers send log lines for genres we're not interested in. Our Web site clearly tells you what we're looking for. When we put out a "call," we tell you exactly what we are looking for. Why would I want to read through all your log lines? I won't read any of them if you make my job more difficult.

- If they ask me to go to their site, I'm not going to do it. The reality is we are not going to go to your site. I print e-mails out and sit down and read them. I don't read them from a computer.

- I'm going to give some preference to those who follow instructions. For example, I posted on *hollywoodlitsales.com* that we were looking for scripts and asked everyone to place "RE: Hollywoodlitsales" in the subject header, and only about 20% bothered to do it. Writers need to pay attention to details. If they can't pay attention to details when querying, how well do they do it in their script?

- Don't grill a real company about being legitimate. That's a turnoff. Sure, there are unscrupulous companies, but writers should keep a paper trail and, of course, always copyright the material. If they do, they don't have a lot to worry about. We expect agents we haven't worked with before to want company information, and we provide it, but we can't do this for every writer that queries.

- Some writers take it too personally when we do not ask to read their script. Some even get pissed off.

It's tough for writers out there.

Yeah, it is. I know; I'm a writer at heart. But there are some writers who have been submitting their material for way too long. They are bitter, burned out, distrustful, and disenchanted. And honestly, I guess, who can blame them? But they come across as unprofessional when they let their frustration get the best of them. That won't get them anywhere. Like I've been saying, we want to see the material first, before anyone else. And we want a good reputation with writers. It's to our benefit to work closely with writers. We want writers to like and trust us.

You can find Script Star on the Web at: *scriptstar.com.*

CHAPTER ELEVEN

A FINAL NOTE

"Hope is a good thing, maybe the best of things, and no good thing ever dies."

— Frank Darabont (*The Shawshank Redemption*)

You're a housewife in Kalamazoo, Michigan; a bartender in Orlando, Florida; an insurance adjuster in Dayton, Ohio; or maybe a high-school dropout working odd jobs in Lexington, Kentucky. You aspire to be more. You have a passion to write, but until now had no idea where to start. After all, "Who am I?"

Well, by now I hope you do have an idea. No matter where you are, nor how unattainable or unimaginable your goals may seem, you are now one step closer to them. The Internet can help you.

As sure as I am that the Internet can help, I'm even more positive that it will be a long and difficult journey. You will need patience and plenty of it. You will develop thick skin, or you will wither under the criticism and rejection.

This book contains the instruction and guidance you need to help you formulate your strategy. Whether you need to do research for that first spec, or you're ready to contact agents and producers, you now have some ideas on where to go and how to get started.

NO EXCUSES

Just a few years ago, if you wanted to be a screenwriter and you were serious about it, you had to move to L.A. And if you were a housewife, a businessman, or anyone without the means to travel West, you were almost always out of luck.

Today there are no excuses. You can't lay back and say, "If only I had connections, I coulda been a contender." You can't hide behind your circumstances anymore. You must have the commitment and desire to make it happen. The Internet is simply a device to help you succeed.

I wish you the best of luck. Please feel free to contact me along the way: *editor@screenwritersutopia.com*.

GLOSSARY

ATTACHED — A producer will often option a script, and *attach* himself to it. This means he/she is now a part of the project. If your script gets made into a movie, this person will be involved. Can also refer to actors and directors.

COVERAGE — A *reader* will critique your script and either recommend it to the boss or not. The recommendation comes in the form of a written *coverage* report. Generally this report is made up of a *log line*, a *synopsis* of the story, and the reader's comments.

DEVELOPMENT —You have sold your script, and now you get to sit back and watch it be systematically destroyed by countless rewrites and changes. Well, hopefully not. Development means that the script is being worked on.

DEVELOPMENT HELL — Your script has gone to hell, meaning that the project is struggling to find financing or distribution, or is still in the *development* stage. There are even more possible reasons, but the bottom line is that the *project* is still in serious doubt. It could get a *green light* — to the filming stage — or it might never get made.

GREEN LIGHT — When your script ceases to be in *development* and goes into production.

HEAT — Also known as "buzz." You want your script to get hot. This means your script is getting a lot of positive feedback from the executives and producers who your agent submitted it to. A script can also generate *heat* when a star is interested or *attached* to it.

HIGH CONCEPT — A universally understood and powerful description of your story. For example, "*Die Hard* on a bus" would describe the movie *Speed*.

LOG LINE — A one- or two-sentence description of your script that should be very simple.

MOW — A television Movie of the Week.

OPTION — An agreement renting the rights of a script for a specific period of time.

PITCH — You *pitch* your story whenever you are talking to someone about it in hopes of generating interest.

PREMISE — A very basic idea representing what the story is about. It often takes the form of a question or a problem.

PROJECT — Your script is a *project*. Always talk about it as such. When someone asks you, "What project are you working on?" your reply should be something like this: "Well, I have this marvelous idea for a script...." You get the idea.

READERS — These are the lucky souls who get to reject your script. A reader is usually an experienced writer. A *reader* will perform what is called *coverage*.

SPEC SCRIPT — A script written *on spec* means you are not being paid up front for it. It is your original script, which you are submitting on the "speculation" that it will sell.

STORY LINE — See *log line*; it is essentially the same thing.

SYNOPSIS — Summary of a story told in the present tense. It should be no more than a few paragraphs in length.

URL — It's the address of a Web page (don't worry about what it stands for). Example: *http://www.whatever.com*

WGA — Writers Guild of America.

SELECTED BIBLIOGRAPHY

Beato, G. "Box Office Bombs: Moving the Hollywood Screenwriting Business to the Internet has Become a Long Soap Opera." *Business 2.0* (Aug. 22, 2000).
Web: *www.business2.com/magazine/2000/08/17947.htm*

Berkowitz, Ben. "Sell Script on Web? Well, the Odds Are Better Than Powerball." *Inside.com* (Jul. 14, 2000).
Web: *www.inside.com/jcs/Story?article_id=6733&pod_id=10*
    (requires membership to view.)

Boorst, Terry, and Todd, Deborah. "Cyber Internetworking: A New Generation of Literary Representatives Surf the Web for 10 Percent." *Written By* (Nov. 2000).
Web: *www.wga.org/WrittenBy/1100/alt.html*

Braunstein, Peter. "Imperfect Pitch: Online Screenplay Ideas Underwhelm Sundance." *L.A. Weekly* (Feb. 4, 2000).
Web: *www.laweekly.com/ink/00/11/cyber-braunstein.shtml*

Chetwynd, Josh. "Filmmakers Getting Discovered Online." *USA Today* (Jun. 7, 2000).
Web: *www.usatoday.com/life/cyber/tech/cth709.htm*

Field, Syd. *Selling A Screenplay: The Screenwriters's Guide to Hollywood.* New York: Bantam Doubleday, 1989.

"Get Discovered.com." *Wired* (Dec. 9, 1999), Wired news report.
Web: *www.wired.com/news/print/0,1294,32987,00.html*

Gordon, Devin. "Trolling for Fresh Ideas." *Newsweek* (Dec. 6, 1999). Arts & Entertainment.

Graser, Marc. "Hollywood Solicits Scripts online." *Variety* (Sept. 1999).
Web: *www.variety.com (requires membership to view.)*

Kennedy, Dana. "Screenwriting @ Your Fingertips." *New York Times* (Jan. 9, 2000).
Web: *www.nytimes.com* (requires registration to view).

Ledbetter, James. "The Web Gets 10 Percent." *The Standard* (Oct. 18, 1999).
Web: *www.thestandard.com/article/0,1902,6991,00.html*

Levy, Frederick. *Hollywood 101: The Film Industry*. Los Angeles: Renaissance Books, 2000.

McHugh, Kenna. *Breaking into Film*. Peterson's, 1999.

Morris, Bonnie Rothman. "Screenwriters Find a Toehold on Net." *New York Times* (Jan 14, 1999).
Web: *www.nytimes.com* (requires registration to view).

Ortega, Tony. "Breaking In." *New Times Los Angeles* (Jun. 1, 2000). Web: *www.newtimesla.com/issues/2000-06-01/feature.html/page1.html*

Phillips, Vicky and Yager, Cindy. *Writer's Guide to Internet Resources*. New York: Macmillian, 1998.

Press, Skip. *Writer's Guide to Hollywood Producers, Directors and Screenwriter's Agents*. Rocklin, CA: Prima Publishing.

Rose, M.J. "The Net Effect on Moviemaking." *Wired* (Dec. 7, 1999).
Web: *www.wired.com/news/culture/0,1284,32773,00.html*

Suppa, Ron. *The Business of Screenwriting*. Los Angeles: Lone Eagle Publishing 1999.

Taylor, Thom. *The Big Deal: Hollywood's Million-Dollar Spec Script Market*. New York: Quill, 1999.

ABOUT THE AUTHOR

Since the early 1990s Christopher Wehner has been working the Web as a screenwriter, editor, reporter, publisher, designer, and manager. In 1995 he founded *The Screenwriters Utopia*, which has grown into one of the most popular and heavily visited Web sites for writers on the Internet. Chris has been the Web editor for *Creative Screenwriting* for the past two years. He has also served as editor and publisher of *Story Crafting: The Fiction Writer's Magazine* and *The Screenwriter's Monthly Newsletter*. Chris lives and works from the mountains of Colorado as a respected monthly Internet columnist covering Hollywood and screen-writing. His writing has appeared in such publications as *Creative Screenwriting* and *Screenline*, as well as on many writing Web sites.

THE WRITER'S JOURNEY
2nd Edition
Mythic Structure for Writers

Christopher Vogler

See why this book has become an international best-seller and a true classic. First published in 1992, *The Writer's Journey* explores the powerful relationship between mythology and storytelling in a clear, concise style that's made it required reading for movie executives, screenwriters, scholars, and fans of pop culture all over the world.

Both fiction and nonfiction writers will discover a set of useful myth-inspired storytelling paradigms (i.e., "The Hero's Journey") and step-by-step guidelines to plot and character development. Based on the work of Joseph Campbell, *The Writer's Journey* is a must for all writers interested in further developing their craft.

The updated and revised 2nd Edition provides new insights, observations, and film references from Vogler's ongoing work on mythology's influence on stories, movies, and man himself.

Christopher Vogler, a top Hollywood story consultant and development executive, has worked on such high-grossing feature films as The Lion King *and* The Thin Red Line *and conducts writing workshops around the globe.*

$22.95
Order # 98RLS
ISBN: 0-941188-70-1

MYTH AND THE MOVIES

Discovering the Mythic Structure
of 50 Unforgettable Films

Stuart Voytilla

Foreword by Christopher Vogler
author of *The Writer's Journey*

An informal companion piece to *The Writer's Journey, Myth and the Movies* applies the mythic structure Vogler developed to 50 well-loved U.S. and foreign films. This comprehensive book offers a greater understanding of why some films continue to touch and connect with audiences generation after generation.

Movies discussed include *Die Hard, Singin' in the Rain, Boyz N the Hood, Pulp Fiction, The Searchers, La Strada, The Silence of the Lambs*, and more.

$26.95   Order # 39RLS   ISBN: 0-941188-66-3

STEALING FIRE FROM THE GODS

A Dynamic New Story Model
for Writers and Filmmakers

James Bonnet

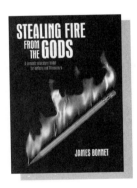

This new state-of-the-art story model will guide professional writers and filmmakers to a more complete understanding of the fundamentals that drive the world's most important art forms: storytelling and film. In the tradition of Carl Jung, Joseph Campbell and Christopher Vogler, James Bonnet explores the connection between great stories and personal growth, and the significance that connection has for screenwriters and other storymakers.

$26.95   Order # 38RLS   ISBN: 0-941188-65-5

FADE IN - 2ND EDITION

The Screenwriting Process

Bob Berman

A classic used by professionals and universities around the world, *Fade In* is a concise, step-by-step road map for developing a story concept into a finished screenplay. Besides learning the basics of screenwriting – from structure to terminology – readers will also glean valuable tips on the realities of breaking into the screenwriting "biz" and how the whole system works, from getting an agent to making deals.

$24.95   Order # 30RLS   ISBN: 0-941188-58-2

SCREENWRITING 101
The Essential Craft of Feature Film Writing

Neill D. Hicks

Hicks, a successful screenwriter whose credits include *Rumble in the Bronx* and *First Strike*, brings the clarity and practical instruction familiar to his UCLA students to screenwriters everywhere. In his inimitable straightforward style, Hicks tells the beginning screenwriter how the mechanics of Hollywood storytelling work, and how to use those elements to create a script with blockbuster potential without falling into clichés. Also discussed are the practicalities of the business: securing an agent, pitching your script, and other topics essential to building a career in screenwriting.

$16.95
Order # 41RLS
ISBN: 0-941188-72-8

....

SCRIPT MAGIC
Subconscious Techniques to Conquer Writer's Block
Marisa D'Vari

Script Magic is a powerful antidote to writer's block that both professional and aspiring creative writers can benefit from. It's based on a deceptively simple principle: if you're not having fun creating your script, it probably isn't going to be any fun to read, either. And if it's not fun to read, how is it ever going to be sold and made into a movie that people will want to spend their money to see?

Using easy and fun techniques designed to tap into the rich creative resources of the subconscious mind, readers will learn how to revitalize their writing and improve their productivity. Create engaging characters, dialogue that jumps off the page, and screenplays that sell!

$18.95
Order # 47RLS
ISBN: 0-941188-74-4

24 HOURS | 1.800.833.5738 | www.mwp.com

THE WRITER'S PARTNER
1001 Breakthrough Ideas to Stimulate Your Imagination

Martin Roth

The Writer's Partner is as reliable and indispensable as its title implies. Whether you're looking for inspiration for new plotlines and characters or need help fleshing out your characters and settings with depth and detail, this book will help you turn your script into a strong, memorable work. It's the complete source to turn to for help with whatever is lacking in your screenplay or novel.

Sections on character development, theme, conflict, crisis, and suspense-generating devices will teach you how to structure your story for maximum emotional effectiveness, *The Writer's Partner* even goes a step further than most screenwriting books: it not only helps you construct a plot, but also shows you how to add color and texture to make your story unique, give it resonance, and create a highly desirable script for producers and directors.

The book covers every major genre, from action to suspense to comedy to romance to horror. Find interesting occupations and settings for your characters, then learn how to flesh them out with realistic dialogue and authentic details. With *The Writer's Partner*, you'll feel like you're in a roomful of talented writers helping you to perfect your screenplay – and you don't have to share screen credit or split the profits!

Martin Roth wrote TV scripts and several best-selling books, including The Crime Writer's Reference Book.

$19.95
Order # 3RLS
ISBN: 0-941188-32-9

FREELANCE WRITING FOR HOLLYWOOD
How to Pitch, Write and Sell Your Work

Scott Essman

Do you read movie reviews or feature stories on your favorite artists and think to yourself, "I could do that"? Have you ever wondered how you can turn your love of movies and pop culture into money in your pocket?

Freelance Writing for Hollywood is your guide to the vast and varied field of entertainment writing. This book provides valuable tips and sound advice on everything from constructing a well-written feature to targeting the markets and publications best for you. Topics range from fundamentals such as defining goals and selecting a medium to advanced subjects such as networking, cold-calling, and self-publishing. Whatever your experience level, *Freelance Writing for Hollywood* will help you find your niche in the field of entertainment writing and give you the tools you need to be successful in it.

$19.95
Order # 48RLS
ISBN: 0-941188-27-2

....

WRITING THE SECOND ACT
Building Conflict and Tension in Your Film Script

Michael Halperin, Ph.D.

Every screenplay needs an attention-grabbing beginning and a satisfying ending, but those elements are nothing without a strong, well-crafted middle. The second act is the meat of your story, where your characters grow, change, and overcome the obstacles that will bring them to the resolution at the end of the story. Consequently, it's also the hardest act to write, and where most screenplays tend to lose momentum and focus. *Writing the Second Act* is designed especially to help writers through that crucial 60-page stretch. Structural elements and plot devices are discussed in detail, as well as how to keep the action moving and the characters evolving while keeping the audience wrapped up in your story.

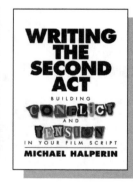

$19.95
Order # 49RLS
ISBN: 0-941188-29-9

THE PERFECT PITCH
How to Sell Yourself and Your Movie Idea to Hollywood

Ken Rotcop *as told to James Shea*

A good pitch can mean the difference between seeing your name on a lucrative studio contract or a form rejection letter. It's a well-known industry fact that film executives typically devote about two minutes of their attention to directors and screenwriters who bring them their ideas hoping for a deal. Can you capture their attention and pique their interest in the time it takes to order a latte at Starbucks? Your future as a successful screenwriter or director may depend on it.

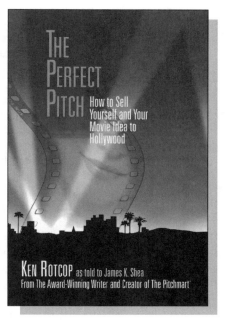

Author Ken Rotcop writes from a unique perspective—he's made hundreds of pitches himself as a screenwriter and producer and heard many more as creative director of four studios. Using personal examples of successes and failures, Rotcop shows you how to walk the tightrope of a pitch meeting without falling off. Which attention-grabbing strategies can make a studio head put down his daily horoscope and listen to *you*? Once you've got his attention, how can you "reel him in" and get him excited about your idea? What if you forget what you were going to say? What if you make a faux pas? Does "no" always mean "no" in the language of movie deals?

Rotcop discusses these situations and others, as well as how to best present yourself and your idea, how and when to do "on-the-spot" pitching, and how to recognize and capitalize on future opportunities.

Ken Rotcop produces Pitchmart™, Hollywood's biggest screenplay pitch event.

$16.95
Order # 14RLS
ISBN: 0-941188-31-0

DIGITAL FILMMAKING 101
An Essential Guide to
Producing Low-Budget Movies

Dale Newton and John Gaspard

The Butch Cassidy and the Sundance Kid of do-it-yourself filmmaking are back! Filmmakers Dale Newton and John Gaspard, co-authors of the classic how-to independent filmmaking manual *Persistence of Vision*, have updated their handbook for the digital age. *Digital Filmmaking 101* is your all-bases-covered guide to producing and shooting your own digital video films. It covers both technical and creative advice, from keys to writing a good script, to casting and location-securing, to lighting and low-budget visual effects. Also includes detailed information about how to shoot with digital cameras and how to use this new technology to your full advantage.

As indie veterans who have produced and directed three successful independent films, Gaspard and Newton are masters at achieving high-quality results for amazingly low production cost. They'll show you how to turn financial constraints into your creative advantage—and how to get the maximum mileage out of your production budget. You'll be amazed at the ways you can save money—and even get some things for free—without sacrificing any of your final product's quality.

Dale Newton and John Gaspard, who hail from Minneapolis, Minnesota, have produced three ultra-low-budget, feature-length movies and have lived to tell the tale.

$24.95
Order # 17RLS
ISBN: 0-941188-33-7

FILM & VIDEO BUDGETS
3rd Updated Edition

Deke Simon and Michael Wiese

For over 15 years *Film & Video Budgets* has been THE essential handbook for both beginning and professional filmmakers. Written by two pioneers of do-it-yourself filmmaking, this book outlines every element of production.

Updated and revised for digital video productions (and video-to-film transfers), this definitive book contains detailed formats and sample budgets for many different kinds of productions, from "no budget" digital movies to documentaries to a $5 million feature—along with all the crucial practical information that's made it an industry bible. Also includes new and highly useful materials, such as a comprehensive master list of line items for just about everything that could possibly be put into a production, and information-packed chapters on handling pre-production and setting up a production company. Also includes Excel sample budget templates downloadable for free from the Web.

Deke Simon and Michael Wiese are veteran filmmakers who have had extensive experience in film, TV, and video.

Budget samples include:
- $5 Million Feature Film
- Documentaries
    (both film and video)
- Industrial
- Music Video
- Student Film
- No-Budget Digital Feature
- Digital Video Feature
- Video-to-Film Transfer
- And more!

$26.95
Order # 9RLS
ISBN: 0-941188-34-5

ORDER FORM

MICHAEL WIESE PRODUCTIONS
11288 VENTURA BLVD., # 821
STUDIO CITY, CA 91604
E-MAIL: MWPSALES@MWP.COM
WEB SITE: WWW.MWP.COM

WRITE OR FAX FOR A FREE CATALOG

PLEASE SEND ME THE FOLLOWING BOOKS:

TITLE	ORDER NUMBER (#RLS _____)	AMOUNT
	SHIPPING	
	CALIFORNIA TAX (8.00%)	
	TOTAL ENCLOSED	

PLEASE MAKE CHECK OR MONEY ORDER PAYABLE TO:

MICHAEL WIESE PRODUCTIONS

(CHECK ONE) _____ MASTERCARD _____VISA _____AMEX

CREDIT CARD NUMBER _____

EXPIRATION DATE _____

CARDHOLDER'S NAME _____

CARDHOLDER'S SIGNATURE _____

SHIP TO:

NAME _____

ADDRESS _____

CITY _____ STATE _____ ZIP _____

COUNTRY _____ TELEPHONE _____